THE
ETERNAL TRIANGLE

THE
ETERNAL TRIANGLE

PASTOR,

SPOUSE, &

CONGREGATION

Robert L. Randall

FORTRESS PRESS
MINNEAPOLIS

THE ETERNAL TRIANGLE
Pastor, Spouse, and Congregation

Cover design: Spangler Design Team

Library of Congress Cataloging-in-Publication Data

Randall, Robert L., 1942–
    The eternal triangle : pastor, spouse, and congregation / Robert
  L. Randall.
      p.   cm.
    Includes bibliographical references and index.
    ISBN 0-8006-2588-9 (alk. paper)
    1. Pastoral theology.   2. Clergy—Spouses.   3. Parishes.
  I. Title.
  BV4013.R36   1992
  253'.2—dc20   91-42375
                                                                          CIP

The paper used in this publication meets the minimum requirements of American
National Standard for Information Sciences—Permanence of Paper for Printed Library
Materials, ANSI Z329.48-1984.   ∞™

Manufactured in the U.S.A.   AF 1-2588

96   95   94   93   92   1   2   3   4   5   6   7   8   9   10

Contents

89069

Preface

THE SUBTITLE OF THIS BOOK—pastor, spouse, and congregation—may sound as if I am writing only to married clergy, especially to Protestant men with wives. Such is not the case in three respects.

First, this book posits that both a masculine and a feminine presence are required by a congregation. The eternal triangle indicates how vital these two presences are in the context of a congregation. When a congregation is headed by an unmarried male pastor, it will seek out a central feminine presence, perhaps a church secretary, nun, or strong laywoman. When a congregation is headed by a female pastor, it will seek out a central male presence, whether that be her spouse, a strong layman, or a denominational leader.

Second, this book can prove insightful to any member of the congregation, whether a layperson, minister, or spouse. Because of the ample discussion of how each corner of the triangle relates to the other two, the reader will almost always find his or her role represented. For example, a congregational leader will understand how he or she functions in relation to the pastor and the pastor's spouse, and a spouse will understand the role the spouse is expected to play in the parish and with the pastor privately. Since these reflections are informed by the self psychology of Heinz Kohut and others, a Glossary is provided to help all readers understand the terms frequently used.

Third, the analysis presented can be applied equally well in Roman Catholic, Jewish, or any other religious group settings, even though I have developed these insights by counseling primarily with Protestant clergy and spouses and by consulting with Protestant churches in conflict. The feedback from non-Protestant individuals who have attended seminars I have led tends to bear this out.

One theme of this book is that each of us needs affirmation from others in order to keep our self secure and striving. I have been blessed with such affirmation during the writing of these pages.

A colleague in the ministry and longtime friend, Larry Randen, lent his editorial expertise and constant encouragement during the early rough draft stages. I felt him reading over my shoulder all along the way.

For the past six years, my pastoral co-worker, Richard Wolf, has scrutinized every page of every book and article I have written before it was sent to the publisher. His insights and good humor have brought me down to earth when my thoughts have taken off into the thin air of abstractness.

Finally, I also want to express appreciation to Stephanie Egnotovich for her professional guidance and for graciously introducing me to friends of hers in the publishing world.

May these printed words thank my affirmers more than I already have.

INTRODUCTION
The Need to Understand and Be Understood

T HE MASKLIKE RIGIDITY of their faces signaled that it had not been a good week.* Nods from each of them served as greeting to me, as though to do more would have compromised their righteous frowns. "He threw my anniversary card in my face," she said sullenly. Her husband shifted uneasily in his seat. "After church we came home and I knew he was upset. When I asked him what was wrong, he wouldn't talk. When I tried to give him my card and a kiss, he brushed me aside and threw it at me. When he gets in that mood I don't know what to do." She leaned back, arms falling limply at her sides.

Her husband countered. "She not only spent Friday night at a wedding rehearsal and Saturday afternoon performing the wedding, but when the bride asked her if she could stay with the groom's children during the reception because they couldn't find anyone else, she said yes. So here on Saturday afternoon I have two strange kids in my house screaming and running around. Neither our time nor our home is ours anymore. It's the church's." Rev. Janice Talbot now shifted uneasily in her seat.

Charles Talbot continued his litany of allegations. "She doesn't manage her work day adequately, she still hasn't learned to say no to parishioners' demands, the kids always seem to come first when she's home, and she's forever tired." Janice started to defend herself, but

---

*All examples have been disguised and are often composites drawn from my years of counseling clergy and their spouses.

1

Charles immediately accused her of not listening to him. Wounded, she retreated again. Winded, and perhaps fearing he had gone too far, he lapsed into a wordless gloom.

After a few silent moments, I turned to him and asked, "Do you begin to feel anxious inside yourself when she's not there to touch you and convey to you that you're wanted and special?"

His eyes moistened. "It's hard for me to say this," he mumbled, looking at the floor, "but I need to have her hold me and for us to make love more often. I get feeling unsettled inside unless that happens. When it doesn't, when she doesn't seem interested in me, I get hurt and then get mad. The card and kiss seemed perfunctory, like she was patronizing me. That made me even more upset. I want her to *really* want to be with me, not just go through the motions."

"And I need you to be strong," she blurted back. "I'm not as sure of myself as you and others seem to think I am. While everyone at church is leaning on me, I'm dying inside for someone to be *my* pillar. When you pull away, I feel terribly unsure. That's why I've tried so hard to make things right, so I could coax you into being that strong person I need. I sometimes think it would be best if I left the church. All I know is I don't have the strength anymore to make you strong for me."

THE CLERGY–SPOUSE–CONGREGATION TRIANGLE

Pastors and their spouses are struggling—with their own individual selves and with each other. Those of us who are pastoral counselors know professionally that ministers and their spouses experience individual and marital problems. As pastoral counselors we also know those problems personally, for each of us contends with our own self and with our husband or wife. No pastor or clergy spouse is immune from becoming emotionally fragmented, nor safe from the danger of marital meltdown.

The parish has always had a profound impact upon the selves of pastor and spouse. It always will, inasmuch as the parish normally approaches the clergy couple with its own emotional needs. Parishes today, however, tend to profess that the minister is a professional whose job is to manage the program of the church, while the spouse is his or her own person, and the clergy couple's marriage is their own business.

However enlightened this view may be, beneath it still surge emotional expectations that the pastor and spouse will be whatever the church needs them to be. At the very least, the parish looks to the clergy couple to bolster the parish's self-esteem, to support its central values, and to promote its community spirit. At the very most, when the well-being of the parish is threatened in some way, the parish relies upon the pastor or spouse to act in ways that will hold the church together and ward off the danger of its falling apart. These are not job description items. They are implicitly operating expectations that pastors and spouses learn about later when problems arise.

The parish also has a profound impact upon pastors and spouses because clergy couples simultaneously turn to the parish for those responses needed to maintain the cohesion of their own individual selves. While pastor and spouse may depend upon each other or past relationships for the approval, soothing, or acceptance they need in order to feel inwardly reassured, they also expect the parish to supply these responses. These expectations, in turn, have a significant impact upon the life of the parish.

This book's title was indirectly suggested to the author by a group of dedicated ministers and their spouses. With all their affection for the church, and for each other as husband and wife, they regularly gather to discuss what they call "the infernal triangle." Their reflections on the difficulties of personal and marital life, especially within the context of the parish, stem from a conscious intention to keep themselves emotionally and spiritually whole and to stay healthily committed to the mission of the church. This book joins with their effort to broaden our understanding of clergy's individual selves, their marriages, and their triangular links with the parish. This book is inspired by this group's firm belief that such hard-won, often painful understanding is worth the effort.

Much tenderness exists in the relationships between pastor, spouse, and congregation. In any serious conversation with ministers, clergy spouses, or parishioners, stories emerge that speak of affection and support for each other. God's care does become incarnate within marriage and within the congregation.

But strains and conflicts are also evident in such stories, and struggles between pastor, spouse, and congregation will be the primary focus. This focus, however, should not be taken as an indication that all is bleak within the lives of ministers, or in clergy marriages, or between the parish and pastors and spouses. The pivotal points of need and the varied reactions are more clearly visible when these central needs are not adequately met and when the firm fabric of personal, marital, and communal life begins to unravel.

The overall intention of this book is to unfold a new, in-depth understanding of the selves of pastor, spouse, and parish, by which our empathy for them and for ourselves is hopefully broadened. The goal is neither marriage counseling for clergy couples nor pastoral consultation with conflicted parishes, but enhancing awareness of relational needs. This in itself can be an occasion of great joy and healing. The pastoral goal of this work, therefore, is not indictment but embracement—the effort to convey a deep sense of understanding so that pastors, spouses, and parishes feel deeply understood. Then is hope renewed, and then does the infernal triangle become an eternal triangle, reflecting God's grace.

THE BOOK'S ORGANIZATION

To enter into the lived world of pastors, clergy spouses, and parishes, some understanding of the nature of the self is needed. This topic is addressed in Part One. Chapter 1 lifts up what we already know about who we are as a self and what we strive for. This implicit understanding is deepened and broadened by new insights into the self that come from counseling work with individuals and groups.[1] Chapter 2, therefore, introduces new terms and views that help us empathize better with pastors, spouses, and congregations.

Part Two examines the inner needs and reactions of pastors and clergy spouses. By deeply resonating with pastors' views from the pulpit, we see how *mirroring, idealizing,* and *alterego* needs shape pastors' relationships with the parish.* By sensitively observing and interpreting pastors' behavior behind bedroom doors, we see how those same mirroring, idealizing, and alterego needs determine how pastors relate to their spouses. We then do essentially the same for clergy spouses. Following our deepened understanding of pastors' and spouses' core needs and expectations, we then look at the various "marriage dances" created by clergy couples. These are the patterned ways of relating that clergy couples establish in an effort to get their central needs met.

A parish is a self, too, with the same central mirroring, idealizing, and alterego needs as a pastor or clergy spouse. In Part Three we look

*These and other terms derived from self psychology are defined in the Glossary.

at this "crowd around Jesus" to understand its emotional makeup. We then consider the various faces of Christ's bride, the church; that is, we see how parishes have their own personalities based upon their core needs.

Our sensing of how we live and move and have our being (Part One), combined with our deepened understanding of the selves of pastors, clergy spouses, and parishes (Parts Two and Three), puts us in a position to empathically interpret those situations where all three are in conflict (Part Four). Here we first consider the story of Rev. Tom Palmer, Mrs. Lois Palmer, and St. Luke's. We see how specific conflicting needs and expectations were the basis of the struggles between them—which they fortunately were able to weather. The second story, in chapter 11, is of a more seriously fragmenting pastor, spouse, and parish, whose hopes for renewal are not as bright.

Every individual, clergy couple, and church has a remarkably strong spirit inclined to reach for help and wholeness. It is part of our created nature to become our best self and to help others be their best selves. In our earlier chapters we witness the self-difficulties that keep pastors, clergy spouses, and parishes from expressing and experiencing fullness of grace. In the chapters of Part Five, we lift up those essential acts that keep individuals cohesive and heal fractured relationships.

A PASTORAL ENCOURAGEMENT

Great joy and comfort can come with learning. Our self-esteem increases when we are in possession of new insights. We feel more in control of our lives. As a consequence, we feel better about ourselves and are thus more tolerant of others.

A part of us, however, resists the unfamiliar and wants to hold on to the customary, even if that is not always helpful. Such holding on is not immaturity but the natural inclination to try to remain cohesive, to try to reassure ourselves when we feel threatened in some way. The terms and ideas we will use to gain a new understanding of the self may seem strange, but they are not. We already know much about them implicitly, in our bones. Furthermore, while not expressed in familiar theological or religious language, these understandings are reflective extensions of our beliefs in how, and for what, God created us. The author himself stands in the community of faith, as well as daily prays for God's guidance in his pastoral work through these pages.

Finally, when we are hurting, we have little tolerance for learning. We simply want someone to make the pain go away, or tell us how we can do so. This new perspective on the selves of pastor, spouse, and parish and on their relationships is as much heart-directed as head-directed. Its aim is to be a means of God's healing power in the lives of pastors, clergy spouses, and congregations—that eternal triangle ordained by God.

PART ONE
Sensing How We Have Our Being

O N E
What Our
Bones Know

Y OU ALREADY KNOW a lot about your "self." You know
it implicitly, through your experiences. You probably
have used different words than the ones we will use to speak about
the self, and you may not have consciously known the broader importance of the self as revealed by these new explanations. But you
are a self, and you already have an in-the-bones understanding of your
self. We begin with that.

AWARENESS OF THE SELF

As you sit reading these words, it would be peculiar for you to say,
or to acutely feel, "I am these hands holding this book," or "I am these
eyes scanning these words." As individuals we exist through our body,
yes, but we sense being more than our body parts or body processes.
In the same way, you do not ordinarily say, "I am these thoughts going
on in my head." You experience yourself as more than just mental
processes, more than just what you are thinking. Similarly, in normal
living you do not exist in a state of depersonalization where you feel
that all you are is the role you play. That may happen from time to
time, as all of us know, yet we typically experience that there is more
to us than the performance of roles.

You implicitly know that there is a more inclusive dimension to
you, something that holds all the parts, processes, and roles together.
We typically refer to this core as the self. Our self is our essential

personhood. It is natural for us to think of our self in terms of a self, by which we indicate the central structure and wholeness of our being.

At certain times each of us becomes "aware of my self," or feels painfully "uncertain about my self." When tragedies occur in our lives, we tend to say, "I feel like I'm losing a grip on my self." If, however, we are surprised by an occasion where people gather to celebrate our accomplishments, we tend to say, "I really feel good about my self." Note the term *my self* instead of the reflexive pronoun *myself.* That's because what these statements really refer to is the self as the central dimension of our existence, rather than just oneself as an object in distinction from others. The points are these: first, prereflectively, without being taught it, you sense that you are a self; and second, you sense also that your self is the nucleus, the core, of who you are.

Fluctuations in Self-Cohesion

You may have noticed something in the statements quoted above. The state of the self—its level of assuredness, its sense of well-being—is subject to fluctuations. Sometimes we feel alive and full of zest. We have energy for our own ambitions, we feel strongly committed to our ideals, and we have deep empathy for the needs and struggles of others. Indeed, at moments we feel like singing with the songster, "I'm sitting on top of the world!" At other times we may feel depressed and limp. Projects and values seem empty, and our capacity for empathizing with others is depleted. It is then, with the singer of the mournful spiritual, that we moan, "Nobody knows the trouble I've seen."

Hopefully you do not regularly swing back and forth between these two extremes, but you know to what I am referring. For example, when your spouse makes love to you warmly, the tensions inside you seem to ease for a while, and you feel more comfortable, confident, whole. When another person gets angry at you and acts coolly, however, your sense of self-assurance can be shaken.

From time to time we all experience some fluctuation in the cohesiveness of our self. We know that is normal. But we are also aware that some people seem able to maintain a generally positive feeling of inner well-being even during stressful times, while other people seem to feel threatened by nearly everything. To say it more precisely, we know persons who experience their selves as firm and consistent, who have positive and reliable self-esteem, whose body, mind, and emotions are balanced and harmonious. We know other people who experience their selves as shaky and always on the verge of falling apart, whose self-esteem is unsteady and easily injured, and whose emotional, physical, and mental activities are listless, excessive, or in conflict. The first group have what we will call "firm self-cohesion." The second have "weak self-cohesion." There are varying degrees of self-cohesion between these two extremes, of course.

Hopefully your self has healthily developed so that you feel basically strong and resilient. If so, then you tend to bounce back to your normal state of firm self-cohesion after encountering difficulties, rather than experiencing your self "fragmenting" in serious ways, which means losing inner assurance and strength to the point where you are not able to function adequately. For instance, if a pastor preaches what she considers one of her best sermons, only to have parishioners give her patronizing comments when shaking hands at the door, her initial flush of confident pride may first give way to doubt, and then later to anger at those who have seemed to take the pastor for granted. It is normal for our inner sense of self-cohesion to be shaken and for us to feel miffed when we fail to receive appropriate recognition for our efforts. If a pastor, however, begins to berate the congregation from the pulpit, or to make threats about leaving, as a result of these injuries to the self, then something more serious is happening. The minister's self is fragmenting, falling apart to some degree, and is in vital need of being shored up. Sometimes we know such fragmentation is temporary. Sometimes, however, we sense that our self is in a state of perpetual vulnerability, where we are chronically supersensitive to disappointments and criticisms.

The point here is this: Not only do you implicitly sense you have a self and that it is the center of who you are; you also know that the condition of your self fluctuates between a general state of cohesion and a general state of disequilibrium. You may not have known this in terms of the exact words and explanations we are using, but you knew it implicitly.

Effect of Others on the Self

What brings about this fluctuation in the self? Why do we sometimes feel so great and other times so lousy? The answer has to do with how responsive we feel others have been to us and how responsive we feel they presently are.

When we experience others approving and appreciating us, we feel confident inside. Our self-esteem builds up so that we are able to healthily affirm our own values and goals and self-perceptions.

When others are reliably available to us to lean on when the going gets rough and we are upset, we feel calmed and fortified inside. As a result, we become better able to soothe our own self when we are alone or hurt.

When others typically convey to us that they are like us and we like them, we feel that we belong, that we are included, that we are connected to others in a deeply meaningful way. Thus we grow in the capacity to assure ourselves that we are normal and acceptable.

What wonderful, life-giving experiences these are! They are the essential experiences necessary for the development and maintenance of a cohesive, harmonized, and vital self. For some of you, these experiences are so naturally present that you take them for granted. Blessed art thou, for these are the roots of your basic sense of well-being in life.

When we are surrounded by "empathically responding persons," we develop the capacity and inclination to be empathic with others. As we are strengthened by the presence of reassuring individuals, we are able to laugh at ourselves and at the foibles of humankind. In the firmness of our self, bestowed upon us and nurtured by supportive others, our creativity juices flow more readily. We experience our self as purposeful and productive. And, peace of all peace, we are able to look at and accept our own dying. In short, when we are surrounded by a milieu of empathically responding others, we not only feel whole and strong inside, but we also become the best self we can become.

If affirmations are absent, however, or we suffer injurious criticisms, then self-doubts arise and our self-esteem wavers. If other people we rely upon to be strong for us pull away from us or act in ways that crush our special image of them, we feel weak and anxiously uncertain. Finally, if other people fail to indicate that they are like us, we feel cut off, alone, and peculiarly different.

These are devastating, excruciating experiences. They happen to all of us to some degree from time to time. No one is immune. When we experience the loss of empathic responses from others, our empathy for others wanes, life seems heavy if not hopeless, our creative productivity stagnates, and death becomes more ominous. For some people, injurious responses from others have been pervasive and consistent. The result is a self that feels chronically vulnerable and empty.

We know how the actions of others toward us affect us. We know how we carry around inside ourselves the memories of being affirmed, which help us keep ourselves going. On the other side, recollections of being painfully rebuffed and alone leave us terribly defensive against being treated that way again. No matter how much we might try to separate our self from others, however, no matter how determined we are to be independent or autonomous, we seem to sense that it is impossible. We know we are reliant on others. From childhood on we have learned in our bones that how we feel and respond is in large measure influenced by how we experience others being for us, with us. The crucial point is that the fluctuations in our self-cohesion are the results of how we experience others affirming or disconfirming us.

REACTIONS TO INJURY
OF THE SELF

Something else happens to us when we feel let down by persons we have relied upon to help us feel good about our self. When we are criticized or disappointed or rejected, we tend to respond by drawing back or by striking out. Injuries to the self lead us to withdraw in hurt or to react with rage. We pull in or punch out.

There is a wide range of depressive withdrawal responses. A pastor's spouse who hears she is displeasing parishioners by what they consider insufficient church participation may feel mildly dismayed and misunderstood. Her private commitment to that church may wane a bit, and she may act quiet at the next church function, but she may still retain basically good feelings about herself and the congregation. On the other hand, a spouse with a vulnerable self, who is hypersensitive to criticism, may withdraw from all church involvements, feel isolated from pastor partner and family, and lapse into a deep melancholy marked by grave self-doubts and even suicidal thoughts.

There is also a wide range of rage responses, from a fleeting frown on the one hand, to obsessive efforts for revenge on the other. For example, Charles Talbot throwing the anniversary card in his wife's face was a response of rage for her injury to his self (she did not provide the affirming acts his vulnerable self expected or demanded). In a less intense form of rage, he might have acted cool toward her for a time. In a more severe form of rage, he might have physically abused her. The point is this: You daily experience, within your self and in the selves of others, some degree of emotional withdrawal or rage when your self is injured.

Self-Restoring Efforts

Although the world frequently does not seem to understand, we know inside that our withdrawal and anger are often our ways of trying to hold our self together. When our self is injured, we do all we can to feel reassured inside. Sometimes we do that by pitying ourselves; sometimes by getting hopping mad.

We all strive in some way to regain our self-cohesion, our inner sense of strength, harmony, and zest for living. The preacher whose self-esteem has been injured by the failure of parishioners to praise his sermon may attempt to reinstate his self-esteem by remembering how he was affirmed as special by persons in the past, or by engaging in some creative activity that is satisfying to him and productive for others, or by immersing himself in comforting communion with God.

Depending upon how devastated the minister is, he may resort to more desperate measures to ward off feelings of fragmentation and to regain self-cohesion. The pastor may engage in private sessions of great self-pity as a way of soothing the hurt and holding self together. The minister may angrily assert himself in a consistory meeting as an attempt to feel reempowered and to restore self-esteem. Or the pastor may turn to his wife sexually for affirmations of his masculinity that he hopes will ward off the pain of self-doubts.

Each of us has certain characteristic ways we go about trying to maintain and restore our self-cohesion, our general sense of well-being. When these fail, we try new ways to get the responses we need, or we may turn to new individuals to find the vital supporting responses. We may even change our self so that we can elicit the affirming, uplifting, or friendship support of important others. Although we may feel overwhelmed, our self seems to keep trying and striving to make its way in the world. In that sense we realize that our self is not passive but active, not weak but healthy and growth-promoting, not simply responded to but the elicitor of responses.

Regaining our equilibrium is indelibly connected with seeking out empathic responses from others. When our self is injured, we basically turn to others to help us reestablish our self's wholeness. We elicit their sustenance; we yearn for, if not demand, their reassuring words or actions. You know when you begin to doubt yourself how a word of praise from a significant person lifts your spirits. You know when you are afraid how an embrace from a strong person calms your soul. You know when you feel left out and strange how a gesture of friendship makes you feel human again.

Sometimes we have an intense, urgent need for people to respond to us so we can hold our self together, leading us to do whatever is necessary to get those responses. At other times we have a more quiet need for people to respond to us so that we can continue to feel adequate. Memories of understanding individuals may be all that is necessary to lift us over a difficult spot in life. The needs of some individuals, however, are chronic—they never seem filled up no matter how much praise or support or inclusiveness is poured out for them.

The points to be made are these: We recognize our active efforts to restore and preserve our self-cohesion when it is disturbed; and we recognize how we search for empathic responses from others so that we can feel safe and restored.

Core Needs

In this storehouse of rich, implicit awareness is one final valuable we want to unpack, namely the central needs of the self. We have already alluded to them. First, do you remember when you were a child how you used to dance and sing and act silly in front of your folks? Or do you remember how excited you were to show mom and dad that beautiful crayon picture you had made in school? In both cases you could hardly wait to see the smiles on their faces or to hear their words of praise. As we look back on it, we take that need to be the center of attention and to be praised as something normal for children. We sense that if children get the applause and words of praise they are looking for, then they feel really good about themselves—often for a very long time. Those admiring responses become the basis for the child's positive self-esteem throughout a lifetime.

If you think about it, you realize that you still want those experiences of being recognized, made special. You sense that you still need "mirroring," as we will call it, that admiration and praise that keeps you feeling confident. While you may not need mirroring responses in the same form you did as a child, you still rely upon them for an inner sense of well-being.

Aren't we supposed to outgrow this need for being made special? a part of us asks. Aren't we supposed to become so secure that we don't need to rely upon others for our self-esteem? Isn't that what being independent means, or becoming an individual means? Look inside your self for the real answer. What does your heart say, regardless of what culture defines as "mature"? It says that we still thrive on the applauding word. We still feel reassured when admired. We still work harder and more confidently when our goals and ambitions are affirmed by significant others in our life. The need for mirroring is normal in childhood and continues in adult life. Implicitly we know we do not outgrow it. We just outgrow some of the ways in which we need to have it expressed.

Similarly, we can sense how from the very beginning we have needed strong comforting figures to run to with our tears and bruises when we have fallen down. We can remember how the reassuring words of mother or father soothed the hurt when kids picked on us, and gave us the courage we needed to go back out and try again. Have we outgrown this need to "idealize," as we will call it, to be lifted up by the word or action of a person we look up to? What does your heart say?

Finally, we can also recall those actions and words from important persons, inside the family and out, who conveyed to us that we were not weird, not an outsider, but that they were just like us and we just like them. How wonderful it was to feel that we belonged and were not left out! Have we outgrown this need for "alterego" responses, as we will call them, for responses from others that make us feel normal and acceptable? Implicitly you know the answer is no. They, too, along with the mirroring and idealizing needs, are a normal part of us, present when we were kids and present with us now as grown-ups. Perhaps we can begin to accept these needs as part of who we are. Maybe we can even accept them wholeheartedly rather than begrudgingly. To do that is to move toward fuller acceptance of this thing we call our self.

T W O
Selves in Ministry

THE IMPLICIT KNOWLEDGE of the self has been characterized with several terms: self-cohesion, fragmentation, empathically responding persons, mirroring, idealizing, and alterego needs.* Hopefully this language feels natural enough to allow for its adoption. A deeper understanding is needed concerning what it means to be a self. To achieve this, a new term, *selfobject* is introduced as a way of describing the power of empathically responding persons in our life. Such "persons" can include not only other individuals but also groups. Thus, both the congregation's and the minister's self play central roles in ministry.

THE SELF OF INDIVIDUALS

A pastor, a spouse, and a parish each has a psychological center called the self. As we shall see later, a parish has a group self that acts similar to the self of an individual. What is most crucial for an individual or a group is the health of the self. When the self is healthy, the person (or group) feels harmonious and balanced inside. He or she possesses positive feelings of self-esteem and responds to others with concerned sensitivity. But when an individual suffers from an empty or vulnerable self, he or she feels internally conflicted and uncertain, is hypersensitive to criticism, and has difficulty responding thoughtfully to others. Stated theologically, a healthy self is the foundation making it possible for

---

*These and other terms are defined in the Glossary.

pastor, clergy spouse, and parish to be the means of grace they are called to be. On the other hand, a vulnerable self is the reason pastor, clergy spouse, or parish are unable to experience and convey the grace they have supposedly received.

Every pastor, spouse, and parish normally needs empathic responses to retain a feeling of well-being within the self. Some of us, like Charles Talbot in our introduction, particularly need admiration and praise; that is, we need mirroring responses from others for what we do and say in order for us to maintain our self-esteem. Some of us, like Janice Talbot, particularly need calming and soothing responses; that is, we need idealized figures with whose strength we can merge in order to maintain our inner security and vitality. Others of us need reassurance that we belong, that we are normal, like others; that is, we need alterego responses in order to maintain our basic sense of being human and of being accepted. These self-needs are not signs of weakness, nor are they sinful. They are part of our created existence.

There is something special in how we experience those persons or groups we look to for mirroring, idealizing, or alterego responses. When we understand this special way we experience them, we will have gained a powerful insight into all human relationships, including that between pastor, clergy spouse, and parish.

Others as Selfobjects

What is crucial for us to understand is that we do not basically react to people as if they were separate from us, as if they were objects distinct and independent from us. We know, for example, that those close to us have their own individual existences and their own private thoughts and plans, yet at the most basic emotional level we experience them as part of us, as extensions of us. Although in the ordinary activities of everyday life they seem to be separate objects with their own space, at the deepest, psychological level we basically respond to them as selfobjects, as part of our own self.

When we were growing up, our parents were our primary self-objects. We relied upon them totally; they were our world, with no distinction between our self and them. How thoughtfully they responded to us, how empathic they were to our needs, determined our sense of how safe life was, how we felt about our self, and what we could hope to expect from others.

Because we had no self-esteem of our own or capacity to affirm our self, we needed them to mirror us, to praise us, so that we could begin to feel positive about our self. Because we had no capacity to soothe our self when upset, they did that for us. Because we had no ability to reassure our self that we belonged and were normal, they acted in ways that let us feel that we were acceptable, like them, connected. Our parents more or less successfully functioned for us, doing for us those physical and emotional things necessary to keep our self strong, hopeful, and soothed. They were psychologically a part of us. We needed, expected, even demanded at times, that they simply be for us in ways that would make us feel all right inside. They were our selfobjects, whose primary meaning in our life was how they served to keep us feeling special, soothed, and assured of belonging.

As we grew up, we became more and more our own person. We began to realize that we were a separate person from mom and dad. We each began to make up our own mind, and to do things our own way, and to have our own identity. That was terribly important in the process of becoming a whole person. What people often fail to realize is that at the same time we were separating, we still continued to experience others as being extensions of us, part of us. We never outgrew our need for others to be our selfobjects. We did outgrow, hopefully, the immature (what we will call archaic) ways we had needed mom and dad and others to respond to us, but our well-being still depends upon empathic responses from others we make part of us. That is not childishness, nor is it symptomatic of persons who cannot stand on their own. It is how we are created; it is how we are bonded together.

A selfobject is not simply a person we depend upon or whom we love. Selfobjects are those individuals or groups, maybe even those animals or machines, that we make part of us, whose response to us we expect will come as we want it or need it. We get a small negative hint of the functioning of a selfobject when, for instance, we feel embarrassed when a loved one does something in public that should really be an embarrassment only to him or her. We may even get mad at the person for making us feel foolish, as though he or she did it not to himself or herself but to *us*. Psychologically the loved one *did* do it to us, for we have made him or her an extension of us, our selfobject, whose grace and wit we take pride in, whose neediness and ineptness we feel ashamed of. Everywhere we look with new eyes we can become aware of individuals responding to others as their selfobjects, as if the very being of others was intimately linked to the heart and soul and well-being of the individual.

Selfobject relationships are vital for all of us throughout life. Our selfobject relationships make us who we are. Who we become is shaped by the responses from our selfobject figures—in the past and in the present. If our selfobjects have responded empathically, we tend to develop healthy self-esteem and firm self-cohesion. But if our self-objects have responded unempathically, or been absent, then we suffer feelings of vulnerability and self-doubt. The normative, central psychological relationship of all human life is the experience of the relationship between a self and his or her selfobject figures. The relationship between a person and those figures who serve as that person's selfobjects is the bedrock of the person's existence. God, it seems, has created us to be indwelling with each other in this special way.

Selfobjects in Ministry

The concept of selfobject is crucial to the discussion of the eternal triangle because every pastor, spouse, and congregation basically responds to the other parts of the triangle as a selfobject. Much more is going on in their relationships than simply "You do your job and I'll do mine," or "Each of us has our own ideas and we'll have to compromise," or some other way of thinking that treats people as separate, rational billiard balls that sometime come in contact for an agreed upon purpose and then return to their own space. We constantly embrace the other as someone or something that we need, expect, or demand will help us enhance our life if not ward off threats to our self-esteem.

When the self-needs of the pastor, clergy, spouse, or parish are adequately met by empathic selfobjects, the pastor, spouse, or parish experiences an inner sense of well-being. For example, when a minister receives praise and affirmation from the parish, his or her goals feel vital and energizing; the pastor's values and ideals feel important and reassuring; his or her contacts with others feel like true sharing and intimacy.

However, when the pastor, spouse, or parish fails to receive empathic responses from their selfobject figures, or the responses are disappointing, the pastor, spouse, or parish begins to feel empty and unsure. For instance, if the pastor's good efforts go unnoticed or are criticized, the pastor may become depressed to some degree, or may lash out at those unempathic persons who have failed to respond as he or she expected. Self-esteem then wavers. Ideals and idealized persons once looked up to no longer seem so special. Feelings of isolation if not abandonment set in.

The basic point is this: The individual struggles of the pastor, clergy spouse, or parish, the tensions in clergy marriages, and the explicit strain in the triangular relationships between the three are all reflections of core difficulties in the self of each, and of core conflicting ways in which each needs the others to fulfill their expected selfobject roles.

In the case of Rev. Janice and Charles Talbot, they both experienced individual difficulties in maintaining a cohesive self. Charles felt devastated when he did not receive assurance of being special and important from his wife. Lacking the capacity to maintain his own self-esteem, he turned to Janice to provide the attentiveness he needed to ward off self-doubts and to regain a feeling of inner well-being. When she failed to be confirmingly available to him in the manner and frequency he wanted—that is, when she failed to be the mirroring selfobject he expected—he became despondent and enraged.

She, likewise, needed him to shore up her shaky and beleaguered sense of self. When she experienced him as a strong, calming person with whose strength she could feel personally fortified, she felt inwardly soothed. Her energy and enthusiasm for the tasks ahead returned. When he failed to function in this empowering way for her— that is, failed to be the soothing idealized selfobject she expected— she fell back limp again. Each self needed the other to serve as their support, inasmuch as each had difficulty maintaining their own self-cohesion and self-esteem.

In the stories to follow, we hear of pastors, spouses, and parishes yearning for empathic responses from each other, and of the injuries they experience when the others fail to fulfill their selfobject roles. That failure creates the infernal triangle. Our purpose is to help bring healing through broadened empathic understanding, so that the life between them becomes the eternal triangle of support and grace.

THE CONGREGATION
AS A SELF

An older colleague returning for further seminary study proposed a dissertation on the subject of personalities of parishes. His sociologically minded professor informed him, "You can't apply individual psychology to complex, heterogeneous groups." Well, just ask any pastor or clergy spouse if churches have distinct personalities and you will see their faces light up (or grimace) in the affirmative. One denominational official said, "It's very strange. You can completely change the cast of characters and still the church remains the same. It's like there are ghosts in the pews and pulpit."[2] This is a way of saying that implicitly we sense there is such a thing as a group self.

A parish is a self analogous to the individual self. The parish group self is the parish's psychological core, that complex makeup of identities, inclinations, levels of tolerance, and sensitivities that are organized into a whole and that organize all other experiences of the parish. The parish has the same needs for mirroring, idealizing, and alterego responses as does the pastor or the clergy spouse.

A church likewise relies upon the presence and power of selfobject figures to hold it together and to enhance its self-esteem. The primary selfobject for the church is the pastor. Our opening story about Janice and Charles hinted about the selfobject expectations of the parish, represented by the attitude of the bride who had no second thoughts about asking her pastor to be a baby-sitter. The pastor was expected to function in ways that facilitated and served the life of the congregation and its parishioners. The parish as a group self also expects the pastor's spouse to act in similarly supportive selfobject ways.

Even though parishes are more aware today of the needs of ministers and their spouses, and even though they may not be as socially and ecclesiastically insistent on personal behavior as an indispensable feature in performing the role of pastor, each parish still expects its pastor and related spouse to serve as its mirroring, idealized, or alterego selfobjects. As long as the pastor and spouse fulfill these expectations, the parish retains self-esteem and group vitality. But should the pastor or spouse fail to provide the kind of mirroring, idealizing, or alterego responses the church expects or demands, the church experiences that as an injury, its cohesion becomes shaken more or less, and it tends to respond with varying degrees of despondency or rage toward its flawed selfobjects.

Each parish has its own quality of self-cohesion. The more vulnerable the parish's self-cohesion, the more sensitive it is to ridicule, rejection, and criticism. The more firm the group's self-cohesion, the more it is able to stay internally solid and to respond empathically to pastor and spouse—even when it undergoes blows to its self-esteem. We now have a formidable tool by which to understand the meaning of a parish's reaction to the behavior of an individual or group.

Self-Selfobject Relations

This deepened understanding of the self allows us to grapple with our individual, marital, and parish experiences in three new ways. First, we are given a new way of observing and interpreting our relationships. Our insights into our self and others are sharpened when we see that a person basically relates to another not as an object separate from the person, but as the person's selfobject. Second, insights into the needs of the self help us become more understanding and accepting of others and of our self. Third, new insights and enhanced empathy give us a wider range of responses to others, along with making our responses more effective.

The essential restoration of human relationships is basically the restoration of self-selfobject relationships. Any serious effort to understand and help individuals and groups must necessarily grasp the power of the self's need for empathic selfobject responses.

Self-Needs in Ministry

When we talk of the self-selfobject relationship being the primary one, we are pointing to the essential relationship that goes on in the ministry between the pastor, clergy spouse, and parish. The joys in these relationships, the grace shown, are expressions of healthy selves functioning for each other in supportive selfobject ways. The friction in these relationships and the pain inflicted are expressions of struggling selves who are failing to find in each other the supportive selfobjects they need. That was the basis of the problem Rev. Janice Talbot and Mr. Charles Talbot had individually and with each other. It was also the basis of the struggle she was having with her parishioners, who expected her to be their consistently available selfobject.

Hopefully it is becoming clear that we are not simply talking about being nice to each other. We are not even talking about how we need to love one another. We're talking about deep psychological needs for experiencing others as part of us, whose empathic responses are the mainstays of our self-cohesion, our self-esteem, and our empathy for the next self. When our self is made firm through the empathic responses of our selfobjects, past and present, we are then capable and inclined to love others fully and to show them the same empathic considerations. On the other hand, our insensitivities and our hurting of others emanate from our weakly structured or fragmenting self.

That does not mean we do not have to take personal responsibility for our actions. We do. But our actions are more than simply a matter of will, and our understanding of what happens in human relationships is deeper than the simple formula "They did this to me." Our actions and ethics express the intricate, mutual influencing of our self-selfobject relating.

Hopefully you are also beginning to feel positive about this idea of self. It certainly has nothing to do with selfishness or egotism. The self we are talking about, namely our psychological core, is of the highest order. Considering the self as our center does not lead to forms of cultural narcissism, to what has been tagged the me-generation. It does not diminish our faith nor our reliance upon God. The self and its nuclear requirements for well-being deserve to be redeemed by the larger church, especially for the well-being of pastors.

Ministers are taught that while "in word and gesture you stand for the most hopeful message it is possible to convey to man," the high dignity of ministry "will derive not from you but from your message."[3] Theologically and ethically we know the important distinction being conveyed here, but sooner or later we need to accept that the word and gesture of the minister are inseparable from the whole self of the minister. A minister cannot have a full, incarnational ministry by going off to a church with just his word and gesture, any more than a penis and vagina can go off to a cabin and have a full, meaningful relationship. Like it or not, in both cases a self is attached. Stated succinctly but with great affirmation, the self is central in ministry.

Pastors complain, of course, even from the pulpit, about the dangers of ego, that personal interests get in the way of God's work. "Not my will but yours be done" is the espoused goal, and rightly so. But the self of the pastor is always centrally involved, and the basic self-needs of the pastor are always normal. It would be misleading to say that the self-needs of the pastor are inevitable, which suggests they are unfortunate impurities of our finite nature. No. Even in the pulpit, the pastor has normal and healthy needs for mirroring, idealizing, and alterego responses. That "high and lifted-up" place does not negate these needs, although that place may modify the form or intensity of self-need expression.

Moreover, the self of the pastor is pastorally indispensable. That is, the pastor's role as God's ordained servant is carried out through the self. The self is not only personal but professional. What the pastor presents to others is the self, and it is through this self that something of God's grace in life is manifest. This, too, should not be designated as inevitable, as though the self is but that imperfect vessel through which God's divine word somehow manages to come through. Instead, the self is God's way. The self is part of God's created order, and through it, as through all aspects of God's created order, does God speak and reveal divine intentions.

PART TWO
Understanding Pastors and Spouses

THREE
Pastors in the Pulpit

WHAT GOES ON DEEP within the pastor when he or she steps into the pulpit is often as much a mystery to the preacher as to the parishioner. In this chapter we attempt to understand the inner experiences of ministers, and to help ministers understand their own selves, by carefully considering the underlying needs that wrap themselves around ministers' hearts. More particularly, we will see how specific selfobject needs and various fluctuations in a pastor's self-cohesion are major factors shaping the pastor's relationships with the parish.

Our central theme throughout is this: the self-esteem and inward cohesion of the pastor are sustained by the selfobject figures he or she is fortunate enough to find and stay connected to. This psychological need for selfobject responses is normal, and the search for sustaining selfobject figures goes on largely beyond conscious awareness. The pastor does not typically wake up one morning and say, "Boy, I'm feeling kind of uncertain about my self today. I think I'll run over to the church and see if I can get someone to say a good word about my sermon last week to help perk up my spirit." And yet the minute I write this, I am aware of having had similar half-shaped thoughts many times. When it seems that the world is passing me by, with other colleagues becoming well-known in clergy circles, then I fantasize, for example, how great I would feel if officials of my denomination called me, earnestly asking me to write a book that would be distributed to every minister.

Everyone reaches out for a physical or verbal hug from someone when their emotional tank feels empty. Customarily, however, when the individual is adequately sustained by supportive persons and his or her self is firm and full, this need for empathic selfobject responses operates as a silent, almost taken-for-granted background in daily experience. It is only when one's self-cohesion is chronically vulnerable or becomes temporarily shaken that the need for restoring acts becomes a foreground experience—and a crisis. It is then that the person becomes hypersensitive to being slighted, ignored, or criticized. It is then that the person reacts with expressions of outrage or with depressive withdrawal.

MIRRORING NEEDS

Let me start with a personal experience. It is a great source of pride to me that people still talk about one particular sermon I preached years ago. When they bring it up, I respond appropriately by expressing a thankfulness that it was helpful, but inside I say to myself, "Man, was that good or what!" I bask in these comments. They make me feel special, endowed with wisdom and skill, ready to produce something else that will be similarly well-received. When a sermon I preach does not elicit great responses, or evokes critical remarks, the memory of having preached this exhilarating sermon helps sustain my self-esteem and keeps me committed to my work and to the well-being of others.

Many ministers are sustained primarily by the mirroring responses they receive. As the pastor stands in the pulpit to preach God's word, she simultaneously presents her self to her parishioners for affirmation and praise. Typically, the minister wants to experience the parish admiring her skills and holding them in high regard. This need for mirroring responses from the parish is normal.

Moreover, seeking affirming responses is a health-maintaining move on the pastor's part. When parishioners pass the word about the helpfulness of preaching, a minister feels appreciated and validated. The enhanced sense of well-being and self-assurance that comes from this admiration fortifies the minister's inclinations to be empathically caring of others. Eliciting and receiving such admiration also helps restore self-esteem when it has been injured in some way. The echo of praise in our heart sustains us when criticisms try to puncture our confidence. Applauding smiles and words often keep us from hemorrhaging spiritually and emotionally. It is normal and healthy, then, for the minister's head to swell from time to time. That is not egotism; it is the flush of pride that the minister needs to keep commitments strong and work energetic.

If the self of the pastor has been firmly developed (through the presence of supportive persons current and past), the pastor will be able to maintain generally good feelings about his or her self when mirroring responses are few. The pastor can be sustained by more quiet expressions of appreciation from parishioners, for example, or by the memory of having been appreciated. The pastor has a solid, inner core of self-esteem that he or she can use to reassure the self and to keep the self from feeling devastated when criticized or taken for granted.

To use our shorthand language of self psychology, the pastor enjoys firm self-cohesion. Indeed, when the self of the pastor is functioning smoothly, with persons reliably sustaining the pastor's self, the need for mirroring assurances from the parish operates quietly in the background. Just as we take for granted the life-sustaining presence of oxygen until it is alarmingly absent, so we take for granted the presence of empathic responses until they are painfully absent.

Injuries to the Pastor

The firmness of the minister's self-cohesion inevitably gives way at times. The self-esteem of a pastor becomes injured when expected selfobjects withdraw or act in ways the pastor experiences as demeaning. The ways in which a pastor may feel the self injured are innumerable, and those ways rapidly multiply in proportion to the self's vulnerability.

Criticisms of preaching or of the manner of conducting worship service are blows to a pastor, for instance, whether they are thoughtlessly made or maliciously intended. Every pastor has heard at the parish door a litany of complaints. "The hymns were too hard to sing. You failed to mention my folks' anniversary. You stand too far away from the microphone. You mispronounced the name of the author. You should be preaching more out of the Bible. How come you don't structure the service like our other minister did?" Outwardly the pastor may stay calm in the face of these comments, but inside he or she probably churns. "They have no conception, no conception at all, about all the details that go into a service," said one minister dejectedly. "They act as if I don't know what's going on or that I don't know how worship should be led."

In the face of such criticism, ministers experience some deflation in their state of well-being. A cloud may hang over the rest of Sunday and its activities. The pastor may want to be left alone. Hopefully that deflation is mild and momentary as the pastor soothes himself or herself by considering the source of the remarks or remembering the beaming comments of the other ninety-nine congregants. But in some cases the criticisms may hit the pastor like the proverbial truck. Whether it was the criticizer's intention or not, the pastor feels run over. Images of being lovingly respected and admired for one's wisdom suddenly seem to wither, leaving the minister apprehensive about the future.

Outrage over such criticisms may likewise be mild and pass quickly, at one end of the spectrum, or it may erupt in hostile, revenge-seeking ways, at the other extreme. One pastor said with grace-saving humor, "Well, we ministers have to get used to being up to our asses in alligators from time to time." Another pastor, who when criticized felt "like a whale who bleeds and then is attacked by everything," could not resist chastising parishioners for their petty thinking.

Pastors also experience blows to their self-esteem when parishioners fail to follow the pastor's pulpit guidance. Getting work accomplished in the church can be very satisfying for a minister. A core of confidence solidifies in the minister from seeing others respond to his or her leadership. A well-functioning parish is a source of pride, a star in the clergy crown even as the pastor thanks God for the congregation's success.

It is often the case, however, that it takes dynamite to get parishes to change. Calls to duty and spiritual encouragement from the pulpit seem to fall on deaf ears, if not stubborn hearts. Parishes continue to act in slipshod and unkind ways even after the minister's best efforts to bring the church around. The pastor frequently takes such noncompliance personally. To some degree, every pastor experiences the resistance to change as a resistance against himself, and experiences the church's continual bunglings as insults to his training and spiritual leadership.

When the parish fails to heed the pastor, the pastor experiences this as lack of respect and tends to respond with degrees of despondency or rage. She may begin to doubt her abilities, to question her call, to wonder if she was really cut out for ministry at all. Depending upon the firmness of her self-esteem, the pastor may lapse into the prevailing status quo or slide into gloomy resignation. Preaching then becomes an empty chore rather than an enlivening event, with the injured pastor preaching "at" disappointing parishioners. An emotional distance may enter into the pastor's words and actions as she withdraws from those who fail to respond to her ministry. Perhaps more than one pastor has found justifying comfort at these times in the words of Jesus: "And if any one will not receive you or listen to your words, shake off the dust from your feet as you leave that house or town" (Matt. 10:14). Pastors engage in much real and imagined dust-shaking as a result of perceived injuries.

A special word is in order regarding the particular injuries to the self suffered by female clergy. On the one hand, female pastors undergo the typical humiliations all clergy suffer, such as being called on the carpet for not visiting someone in the hospital, or being made to explain themselves and their behavior in front of pastoral review committees, or having to combat rumors about their marriage or the character of their children, or having to endure a panel of parishioners who inspect the parsonage and present complaints about the quality of house-keeping.

Beyond this, female pastors' very commitment to ministry is often called into question. Women ministers report the attitude in parish circles, whether subtle or outspoken, that a parish should think twice about hiring a female pastor because when the chips are down she will probably be more dedicated to her husband and family than to the needs of the church. That attitude may become translated into a rigorous scrutiny of how she spends her time, or into a salary package significantly below what a male pastor would earn at a similar church for similar work. One capable woman pastor finally succumbed to all the blows to her integrity and dedicated efforts: "I am dead to the core of my being," she said with dark despondency. "All that I've worked for to become a minister seems like nothing. And I feel like nothing." Not only was her self fragmenting, but her selfobject attachment to the parish was likewise disintegrating—hopefully only for a time.

The need for mirroring response may be the dynamic behind a common cleric complaint. Ministers routinely report that parishes impose intolerably heavy schedules on them. This complaint comes up so often in clergy surveys that it is taken as a bona fide criticism of parishes. It probably is to some degree. But what tends to be over-looked is that this pressure to perform is often equally rooted in a pastor's need to constantly receive validation from selfobject parish-ioners. Consequently, a minister can become caught up in a rapid proliferation of activity because he worries that if he says no to requests, the congregation will stop affirming him. If the minister's self is es-pecially vulnerable, he may strive for near-perfection in his work as a way of eliciting positive strokes or avoiding criticism. "It's not so much that I want others to claim I'm perfect," said one workaholic minister, "it's just that I can't stand to hear that I'm not perfect. Any vibe I get from the congregation that I'm slipping nearly panics me." While parishes certainly sometimes have unreasonable expectations, the compulsive work habits of ministers often stem from their need to have others continually affirm their selves.

All ministers from time to time normally experience injuries to their self-esteem when supportive mirroring selfobject figures are absent, inadequate, or attacking. When this occurs, the pastor's self begins to fragment to some degree; that is, the minister loses the reassuring sense of being whole, balanced, and strong. Self-confidence crumbles a bit. Robust bodies become listless. Alert minds feel overwhelmed. Spiritual assurances become thin. The minister does not make use of people who could help. Irritation turns into rage and a desire to get even. Empathy for others diminishes. Resolves dissolve. Controls on impulses and urges weaken.

Chronically Vulnerable Pastors

Some pastors suffer from chronically vulnerable self-cohesion, as we have suggested in previous examples. They have a difficult time maintaining their own self-esteem under any condition. They constantly need applause and praise from others to feel confident and to keep functioning. They have, in essence, come to the parish with archaic selfobject requirements and expectations.

If, for example, mirroring needs are excessive, the minister may expect near-total agreement from parishioners for everything he proposes. One pastor could not shake a militant, I'm-in-charge posture. "After my sermons I want them to get on the stick, hop to it, be perfect, know the truth and do it." The truth and action, however, were basically as he construed them to be. He was enraged, consequently, when the congregation did not follow his directives for church policy. Nonresponsiveness was a slap in the face to him. In other words, he related to the parish as if it were an extension of him, his selfobject, which he expected to function in ways that would infuse him with the self-assurance he lacked. Prompt compliance momentarily confirmed for him that he was a good minister; resistance and rejection of his guidance endangered his fragile hold on his self.

Preaching, therefore, may be that occasion by which the pastor looks for those intense mirroring responses needed to keep the self functioning at a basic level. The selves of some pastors are weakly put together and prone to fragmentation. The pulpit, then, becomes that central "high and lifted up" place from which the minister leans for the affirmation that will help keep the self glued together—for the moment. Preaching can give the illusion of being in control, and so momentarily empowers. It lifts the pastor into prominence, countering the experience of being helpless, belittled, or ignored. The preacher may resort to an authoritarian tone in the pulpit to protect the self, and to engender feelings of being strong and forceful. Anger disguised as righteous indignation may justify striking out verbally at those who have offended. In an old story, a minister makes a marginal note in his sermon that reads, "Weak point, preach loud." How descriptive that is about some pastors who privately feel weak but "preach loud" to feel strong.

Preaching may also be experienced as a threat. The minister may fear that he will be exposed from the pulpit as weak in the faith, an emotional phony, or basically unlikable. The anticipation of being found out and shunned may lead to a severe restriction of expression. The self and its boundaries shrink until an activity like preaching becomes rigid and narrow in style. The minister does what is safe from the pulpit, delivering sermons that lack a sense of the pastor's personal involvement. One injury-sensitive pastor could share nothing of his personal faith or normal human struggles in sermons, feeling that self-revelation was exceedingly dangerous. "There is never in my sermons any personal references. That's not just because I've been taught to preach that way. It's because I don't want anyone to know too much about me. I don't want to make myself vulnerable to personal rejection. If they reject anything it will be rejection of God's word, because that's all that I give them." As a consequence, his circumscribed self could not reach out from the pulpit or at the bedside of the ill with that personal touch so longed for by parishioners. Unfortunately, fear of rejection also limited his opportunity to grow as a person and as a pastor.

Do not suppose that all ministers with fragile selves appear weak or recognize their vulnerability. Many simply disavow their reliance on mirroring responses. In fact, they act grandiose, presenting themselves as full of power and certainty. They preach as if they know the truth and have been personally selected to proclaim it. One pastor's sermons were riddled with aggrandizing statements. "Now listen carefully to this! Does this mean anything to you? I wonder how much you really listen, how much I say from this pulpit really stays with you. That's the way I see it and that's the way I preach about it." He reminded me of another pastor who declared before the congregation that he should not be addressed by his first name, for he was set apart by God to save their souls. Thus, he should be respectfully addressed as "Reverend," as appropriate for his special calling. Both of these men operated from an immature state of self development, but denied there was anything unusual about how they spoke or related to others.

Grandiose-type ministers often become idealized by parishioners, who need to attach themselves to charismatic figures who appear to be super-endowed. The near-worshipful attitude parishioners can have toward their selfobject pastor validates and heightens the grandiosity of the minister. The pastor's self can swell until he feels invincible, beyond reproach, entitled to do whatever he wants. Some of the excesses evident in televangelists of the recent past are examples of grandiose selves expanding until all limitations are deemed nonapplicable.

Seeking Restoration

The person whose self is fragmenting tries to shake off the terribly disturbing feelings and to regain a sense of inner equilibrium. When our cohesion is only slightly disrupted, we can more easily regain our equilibrium by telling ourselves that we'll be all right, or by remembering how we were successful in the past, or by relying upon words of encouragement from someone we respect. If the fragmentation is more severe, we might resort to more intense measures, such as pumping ourselves up with anger, or doing something that will elicit attention from others, or withdrawing into our self for a time. If our self-cohesion is chronically weak, or we are on the verge of total self-disintegration, then we tend to engage in forms of regressive behavior in a desperate attempt to hold our self together. One minister engaged in peeping-tom behavior and excessive masturbation, another in reckless, daredevil driving, and another in prolonged meditation where he experienced himself sitting in the presence of God.

In the absence of sustaining selfobject responses, and in the resulting state of vulnerability and uncertainty, it does not take much for a minister to start feeling sorry for himself or herself. In this mood, the pastor may look around longingly for the touch of a person who can soothe the emptiness and supply an excitement that will rekindle feelings of strength and aliveness. In such situations, sexual affairs that ministers become involved in are not primarily about sex. Instead, they are desperate attempts by the minister to elicit those powerfully reassuring mirroring responses that will ward off the pain of self-disintegration and provide a sense of regained vitality. Sexual involvements in this state are efforts to hold the self together.

IDEALIZING NEEDS

The distinction between the need for mirroring and the need for merging with an idealized person is often clear. For example, one minister stated this reason for selecting me as his pastoral counselor: "I think your personality and mine will match. You're introverted and laid-back, and that's great, because it's going to allow my extroverted ego to take center stage here in therapy, like it wants to." I was to be an admiring audience for his actions in the theater of his therapy. The centrality of his mirroring needs, and the subtle ordering of my mirroring role, were undisguised.

Another clergyman called for a therapy session after he had read my book, *Pastor and Parish*. As our work together progressed, I began to understand that his fragile self longed to be in the company of someone with soothing words and uplifting thoughts, someone he could admire, feel a part of, and thus feel strengthened by. I was to function as an idealized selfobject figure he could merge with in order to bind up his developmentally fractured self. In mirroring, the pastor's sense of specialness is validated and maintained by responses from admiring selfobjects. In idealization, the pastor is fortified and calmed by merging with admired selfobjects.

These distinctions are important. When we relate to someone in one selfobject way while that person is trying to have us relate in a different way, that person feels misunderstood. If with the first pastor I had tried to make myself available as a soothing (idealized) figure when what he needed me to do was reflect his own feelings of specialness (mirroring), my incorrect understanding would have interfered with the establishment of a bond of empathy with him. The establishment of an empathic bond with another person or with a group is the central, critical experience necessary for the strengthening and healing of selves. More about that later. In any case, we care for and nurture others by being attuned to their particular selfobject needs.

Varieties of Idealization

As the preacher steps into the pulpit, his or her self may be held together and motivated by the sense of being at one with revered persons past and present. Many ministers preach empathically and faithfully by remembering idealized individuals with whom they feel an intimate partnership, whose perceived strength, wisdom, and undaunted values they feel united in and with. Often that figure is a parent, youth minister, college chaplain, seminary professor, or renowned evangelist. Once when a group of ministers were reminiscing about cherished persons who had sustained them in ministry, I recited a line from a lovely song to catch the mood of what they were expressing: "If I can fly higher than an eagle, then you are the wind beneath my wings." Tears flowed. Pastors remember and are encouraged by these deeply embedded connections with idealized companions.

In preaching, the minister may deeply identify with those revered persons, sensing that his or her convictions, vocal rhythms, and even hand gestures are molded after the respected model. Preaching may become that occasion by which the minister proclaims those cherished ideals arising from and represented by idealized figures. The minister's capacities to run the race of repeated sermon preparation without growing unduly weary, and to finish the good fight against parishioners' anxious hearts and stubborn minds without growing unduly cynical, are often grounded in this experience of being lifted up into the inspiring lives of these special others.

Then again, a minister also continues to need idealized selfobject support. While not always obvious, it is commonplace for a pastor to rely upon certain parishioners to function in this selfobject way. Even firmly confident ministers are sustained by the presence and wisdom of respected church members by whom they can feel fortified. They find comfort in not having to go it alone. For example, the pastor's concern, if not anxiety, about financial decisions may be assuaged by the composed opinions of parishioners the pastor deems as wise guides.

Certain parishioners may be relied upon as spiritual mentors, whose exemplary life and impassioned words inspire the pastor's faith and keep his or her hopes alive. Pastors frequently express that they are often ministered to by the very persons they come to serve. This sometimes is a surprise; often it is yearned for, for clergy also feel depleted, lose their vision, and become fearful of disease and death. They, too, seek strength and peace from admired individuals. How a special parishioner lives with pain, overcomes obstacles, or meets death courageously can soothe the pastor's own anxious spirit and can give spiritual direction and support for the pastor's own personal reactions and pulpit proclamations.

The pastor may turn to the parish as an idealized selfobject in other ways. New, untried clergy hope to be met with patience and tolerance by the first parishes they serve. Perhaps with some naiveness, they expect that the parish will be a group of gentle, caring Christians who, as one young minister said, "will either applaud my pulpit blunders as humor or excuse them on the basis of my general goodness." More or less consciously, beginning pastors look for the parish to act as a steady holding environment, as a quietly supportive crucible they need while their self is transformed into being and feeling like "a real minister."

Some sensitively responding parishes instinctively provide this nurturing climate for the consolidation of the pastor's new identity. My rural home church was the first parish experience for many ministers. At various church anniversaries these now seasoned pastors return and relate how reassuring that first experience was. "I suppose every minister has a special feeling about his first parish," observed one pastor. "The Zion people were very kind and patient with this young pastor fresh from seminary with little preaching experience." That mature congregation not only encouraged his budding talents (a mirroring function), but in nonverbal ways it also served as a stable and reliable environment (an idealized selfobject function) by which that minister could practice and find his pastoral identity.

A minister may also relate to a particular church as a whole as an idealized selfobject. If a church has been historically prominent in the past, or is currently prestigious due to size, finances, mission, or having been served by renowned clergy, the minister's sense of internal security and well-being may be stabilized through feeling linked with the church's cultural-spiritual specialness. This selfobject connectedness, therefore, may animate the minister's preaching. "I feel the inspiration of former pastors in the pulpit with me, and the presence of parish folk long past," mused one pastor.

Idealization Injuries to the Pastor

A pastor's inner sense of well-being becomes disturbed when expected responses from idealized persons or parishes are absent. It is normal for the minister to experience some degree of despondency or irritation when this happens. "I have come to the point in life where I realize that all my clergy and lay heroes have feet of clay," sighed one minister. "There is no one I can try to emulate; no one who has that outstanding spiritual character I can lean on and learn from. I find little comfort in thinking that all of us in the church are cripples, just limping along the best we can." For a time this minister withdrew into his self. He carried on normal duties but without zest or purpose. That others looked to him for reassuring words from the pulpit seemed ridiculous to him, for there was no one *he* could listen to for the comfort he needed.

Fortunately his loss of self-cohesion was transitory, as it is in many cases. His basically healthy self was able to find alternative ways of drawing strength from these heroes. Yes, they had feet of clay, but that made their accomplishments and their persistence all the more admirable, he now asserted. "They don't have to be without a limp. It's how they *got* the limp and what they *do* with it that makes them inspiring." He reconnected to his supportive figures by re-visioning them, by appropriating them on a more mature level.

The important point, however, nearly lost in the joyful news of his restoration, is that he also demonstrated the normal mourning and despondency that come with some inevitable reevaluation of our self-object figures. Within the church, ministers are always experiencing disappointments in people they have relied upon. Some pastors become cynical, others continually surprised, others worldly-wise. But all experience a thud to the soul when it happens, that let-down feeling when the designated stabilizers of our existence fail us.

If we consider the issue of financial remuneration from this viewpoint of the minister's dependence upon idealized selfobject, we see the basis of a common but often frustrated fantasy. The pastor's idealization tendencies may incline him to see the congregation as an especially caring body. The pastor may assume that his financial needs will be optimally considered and met by the God-loving and people-sensitive parish. He quietly harbors images of economic security provided by the congregation's numbers, financial resources, and tender empathy. The minister's self may be severely shaken, however, when the parish responds in a detached, businesslike way to his financial situation, or is actually stingy, or expresses the desire for the leadership of a minister who is more concerned with serving than with how adequately he is compensated.

Among themselves, ministers often vent great rage about such "uncaring" congregations, to use a mild invective of irate clergy. Most of the time such rage stays in the form of inner thoughts, or spewed words to colleagues, or passive-aggressive acts (e.g., the minister stops working so hard as a passive way of slapping back at the church rather than confronting it directly). But if the pastor's self-cohesion lacks reliable firmness, so that the minister is unable to soothe his self and modulate the rage, he may consider more serious retaliations. Ideals and ethical values at these times may lose their power for self-guidance as archaic rage takes over. One pastor, for example, left the hot water running in all the faucets of the parsonage day and night in order to run up the church's utility bill. Another minister quietly skimmed money from church offerings.

Chronically Weak Pastors

Some pastors are chronically vulnerable. They need constant assurance of being connected with idealized selfobjects, human and divine, in order to curb anxieties and carry on normal functioning. For instance, ministers may preach not only as they are filled with God's spirit, but also in hopes of finding God's spirit, in order to reexperience their selves being infused with divine grace and strength. They preach in order to become convinced of the message they proclaim. They jack up their own emotions, imitating inspiration in hopes of becoming truly inspired.

Similarly, chronically vulnerable ministers may strive mightily to motivate the congregation in order that the congregation might become motivating to the pastor. Some pastors with weakly structured selves are not able to be inspired by, or to put into practice, their ideals and values unless they become involved with others who provide an enthusiasm for those ideals and values. A minister, therefore, may need the congregation to be vibrant of spirit and hopeful of purpose in order for the pastor to experience something of the same. While the minister may act the part of the energized preacher, the strength and zeal he or she exhibits may feel weak if not personally foreign. Strength and zeal only become real to the preacher, or seem authentically empowering, as the preacher experiences them coming from the inspiring congregation.

In more serious states of chronic vulnerability, a pastor may seek to maintain self-cohesion by attempting to merge with the self of another. As we have noted, all of us do this normally to some extent, but the quality of this merging effort is of an archaic nature. It is one wherein the minister more or less "becomes" the person he or she idealizes. The minister in this case often lacks a firm sense of identity, finds it hard to feel like the same person from one situation to another, and is basically unable to soothe and give direction to his or her life. Such a state is intolerable. Consequently, the pastor endeavors to ward off this crisis and to preserve some semblance of being a self by fusing with the values, visions, and mannerisms of an idealized figure. In severe cases, the minister may exhibit a fictive personality, wearing the face and mimicking the words of those heroes he or she has now become.

If the clergyperson's fragile self lacks the internal capacity for self-soothing and steady self-direction, especially in the face of leadership situations that threaten the pastor's self-cohesion, the minister may relinquish a leadership position altogether. Unable to generate enthusiasm for goals and projects, unable to be motivated and directed by his or her own espoused values and meanings, the minister looks desperately for someone whose vision and dedication seem authoritative if not God-sent. The repeated response of one such pastor when asked questions by parishioners was, "I'll have to check with the president of the consistory." From the vacancy within him he literally had no firm opinions, no firm sense of where the church should go or how. He tried to fill that disturbing vacancy by a fusing merger with the council president. In so doing he was not merely borrowing facets of the idealized figure for enhancement of his own growth, but he was becoming the idealized figure in order to soothe his empty, frightened spirit.

There is a decisive difference between the pastor connecting himself to selfobject figures who have values in harmony with the pastor's self, and the pastor abandoning himself to a figure through which he gains cohesion, but at the price of losing genuine initiative and creativity. At times, however, the price must be paid for self-preservation.

Rather than attempting to be one with an idealized person, some ministers are unable to let another's strength infuse them at all. Their merger needs are so intense that they guard against showing any sign that they might need the support of others. They are fearful of being devastated by the responses of others they might turn to, as they have been in the past. A highly intelligent, intimacy-shunning minister put it this way: "All I am is a survivor, a survivor of a psychic holocaust. The emotional air I breathed was like asbestos, lethal. That's all I am, a survivor. I need people desperately, but if I let anybody know this about me I open myself to emotional ambushes." He was not psychotic, just extremely vulnerable to unempathic responses that could once again disintegrate his fragile self.

Empty and desperate though they be, these clergy often project an attitude of non-need, or "keep your distance." George Adam Smith, in a book written a half-century ago on Isaiah, observed that, "Some righteous people have a terrible northeastern exposure; children do not play about their doors, nor the prodigal stop there. The spectacle of one pure heroic character would be their salvation."[4] How well put! If the pastor as a child or as an adult had found one person he could consistently idealize and look up to, one individual that for him was the assured embodiment of goodness, he might have been saved from the despair of sad bitterness and isolation.

ALTEREGO NEEDS

A pastor's self-esteem is buttressed by affirming selfobjects. His or her self is soothed and values strengthened by admired selfobjects. The assurance of belonging, of being normal and accepted, is based on akin selfobjects, called alterego selfobjects. Some members of the clergy derive the sustenance that maintains their selves mainly from feeling surrounded by others they deem as essentially identical to them. They love and work confidently as they sense their selves connected to others whom they experience as basically the same as them, doing similar work, sharing similar attitudes, beliefs, and practices. They are able to endure the inevitable difficulties of life by having someone by their side who shares their common lot.

When others respond as our alterego, this gives us the conviction that our behavior, emotions, and thoughts are normal and that we belong—to particular individuals, to special groups, and even to the human race. Nothing is more painful than feeling disconnected and alienated, a feeling that the absence of a sustaining alterego milieu can create for a pastor. A pastor who enjoys firm self-cohesion can experience a supportive sameness-of-self with a wide variety of people in a wide variety of contexts. But the minister who suffers from weak self-cohesion may need or demand to be in contact with others who are specifically just like the pastor. Only in the presence of narrowly self-same others may the pastor ward off the threat of fragmentation.

Empathic alterego responses may be the central requirement for preserving a pastor's state of cohesion. I remember a morose minister who kept coming to therapy but did not seem interested in any empathy I tried to give him. He quietly brushed aside my appropriate admiration for his accomplishments in the parish (he did not need me to mirror him). He passed over my efforts to uplift him when difficulties arose (he did not need me as a soothing, idealized selfobject). In fact, he did not seem very interested in me talking much at all. Finally I realized what was happening. He was looking for companionship. He was looking to be in the presence of someone he experienced as sufficiently like him, who could understand him, and whom he could understand. He desperately yearned for a warm echo to reassure him that he was linked to something, to somebody, that a human connection was being made. In those moments between himself and a kindred spirit who silently communed with him, his anguished loneliness eased a bit, and for a time his sense of being strangely different diminished.

Normal Needs for an Alterego

Alterego selfobjects can assume a pivotal place in the work of the minister. Looking for relationships with similar others in the parish can be quite normal for pastors. In fact, it is a familiar experience. One minister's work in a country church included these reminiscences: "Jean and I were treated to the traditional shivaree soon after returning from our honeymoon. One evening a large group of church folk sneaked up in the dusk around the parsonage and suddenly broke out with the customary noises. Fortunately, they also brought with them the food for a fun party. It helped us feel as though we belonged."

We did that to one of our newly married ministers when I was a sophomore in high school. As I remember, it not only made them feel at home, but it made me and the others feel at home with them as well. That human touch between pastor and parish remained long after that evening's fun had faded.

It might not have been so, however. No matter how warmly receptive we might have been, the pastor might not have experienced us as alteregos, might not have deemed us as individuals sufficiently like himself that he could feel comfortable with and with whom he wanted to commune personally. But both he and we found in each other sufficient reflections of our own selves, and so we were drawn together. Alterego bonds with the congregation can enhance a pastor's enjoyment of parish activities, can provide a sense of companionship through the struggles of life, and can sustain the pastor's identity when it is sorely tried. We all need such responses. Some clergy with vulnerable selves, however, have pressing and regressive needs for alterego connections.

Intense Needs for an Alterego

A middle-aged pastor conveyed to me that before each Sunday sermon he suffered repeated anxiety attacks that caused him to vomit violently.

As he stood up to preach, it seemed that it was "them" on the one side, and "he alone" on the other. A foreboding fear that something terrible would happen shrouded his spirit.

As we begin to explore the meaning of these pulpit experiences, he recalled how he had always felt himself alienated from others. A physical disability early in life left him feeling painfully different. Because of it he was always chosen last for games, and even then begrudgingly. No one approached him as a friend. No one invited him to their house to play or for parties. On the school grounds and in his neighborhood he felt abnormal. Neither his body nor his emotions seemed like those of the other children. "I was responded to, and felt like, a weird kid." It was devastating to him—not just the loneliness but the exclusion, the deep-in-his-soul feeling that he was cut off and belonged nowhere and to no one. He tried hard to keep feeling good about himself. He worked diligently on his studies and engaged in private activities so he could feel strong and confident, but he was always on the outside socially and thus was always uncertain about himself on the inside. Repeated episodes of not fitting in over the years left him bereft of assurances that he was connected in any significant way to others and that he was normal.

His fragile self lacked supporting memories of being surrounded by others who conveyed to him that they were like him and he like them. His real handicap had not been his physical disability but rather the traumatic loss of alterego others, those whose echo-confirming responses could have grounded in his self the firm conviction of his normalcy, his belonging—his humanity. His self was alterego-starved and vulnerable. It was this yearning for alterego support that psychologically motivated him to enter the ministry. In the parish, he envisioned, there would be a community of sensitive, faithful selves with whom he could identify and who would identify with him. He would finally belong; he could then feel strong.

This longing was quickly demolished in the parish. He had become a pastor for personal reasons rather than functional reasons. "What I wanted so badly was to belong, but what I soon realized was that they expected me to serve, to fulfill the functions of a pastor. There was a gulf between us." Each preaching occasion presented the possibility for reexperiencing those same excruciating experiences of being excluded. As he stood up to preach, he was once again that physically disabled little boy who was sure he would be cast aside as weird and undesirable. In the face of this threat to his whole being, a flood of foreboding anxiety would hit him, which he could not make go away. His whole self began to fall apart, emotionally and physically.

The first sentence in M. K. Bower's book, *Conflicts of the Clergy,* solemnly pronounces: "The clergy are lonely, set-apart people."[5] That is a shaking statement, but one with which many pastors would agree. Some remember loneliness in childhood that continues into adult life and work. Even healthy and fulfilled pastors talk of the loneliness of the ministry, as if that were a given occupational hazard. Whatever its origins, the experience of set-apartness is terribly painful and ultimately intolerable. One solution, as we have seen, is to look to the parish for those missing alterego embraces. At times the pastor simply assumes that the alterego bonds are readily available in the parish, as in the case of the man just described. But often the minister makes active efforts to elicit if not create the longed-for alterego connections.

For instance, it is not unusual for clergy to attempt to create a set of alterego relationships in which they can experience others as family. One female pastor said, "I have parishioners who respond as mothers and fathers and grandparents to me. It's great!" She found a sense of belonging as she experienced others as kin, as like her in a family system way. Such relationships can be healthy, of course, a healthy re-creation of home life in the context of parish life. We are all familiar with the images and symbols of family ties in our religious language.

Pressing alterego yearnings can lead to excessive efforts to create an extended family. Out of personal need, ministers may attempt to shape worship so that it effects a family atmosphere, wherein the pastor feels warmly connected to others in kinship ways. The pastor may practice folksy approaches to the sacraments, such as carrying the newly baptized baby up and down the aisle, showing the infant off to the congregation while the choir sings in the background. The minister may cultivate informality for the whole service, calling everyone by first names and insisting that others address the pastor only by his or her first name. The congregation may be encouraged to offer prayer requests, or spontaneous prayers, or announcements about the life of the church family. (Even the parish is called a family.) Preaching may be done from out of the pulpit, in a dialogue with the congregation or in a loose, conversational style. In his sermon, one minister boldly declared his intentions: "It hurts me to say that I can't find fellowship today with other ministers, the leadership of our denomination, or with the wider church, and so I've decided I'll have to find it with you." That most definitely was a cry for intimacy and belonging directed to the alterego-perceived parish.

None of these actions just described in itself indicates excessive efforts to create an alterego milieu. Moreover, this whole approach may be appropriate for a parish with alterego needs along the lines of this informal, family style of worship. But the alterego-hungry pastor may force this style upon a congregation that experiences it as foreign or as not what worship is about. The pastor, however, may ignore their signs of discomfort and continue to utilize the parish and worship as the means for overcoming painful memories of feeling alienated.

For some severely impaired pastors, the alterego search is of a decidedly regressive nature. A clergyperson may become inappropriately personal under the guise of being "the minister." Not feeling that she belongs, the minister may latch on intensely to any situation as if she did belong, always in a manner that is overdone. At a funeral or wedding she may speak to strangers in a confidential way that is inappropriate and for which people are totally unprepared. Even with parishioners who know her, she may talk in a manner that is too revealing, too disturbingly intimate. From the pulpit she may carry on the same inappropriate air of familiarity, relating personal matters concerning her finances, conduct, or even sexual thoughts and actions. All the while she remains perplexed when people shrink back from her. The brush-off and distancing, however, are further injuries to her self, leading, perhaps, to even more desperate attempts to preserve self-cohesion by eliciting alterego responses.

A pastor may rely upon particular parishioners for the joy and assurance of alterego belonging. Special relationships may be cultivated with members whose theological outlook, musical interests, sports activities, cultural background, or personalities are like those of the minister. Relationships with parishioners of the opposite sex may also be fostered that are not strictly pastoral, nor strictly man-woman motivated, but more a longing for closeness with a kindred soul. If these relationships do spill over into sexual activity of some sort, they often are not primarily about sexual impulses and drives, but about emotional yearnings to feel whole via intimacy with "someone who experiences things as I do."

Reactions to a Flawed Alterego

As in the frustration with mirroring and idealized individuals, so, too, does the pastor respond with degrees of despondency and even rage at flawed alterego individuals. Pastors with firm self-cohesion will be able to maintain their hope and faith when this happens, however.

Typically they do this by finding alternative alterego figures. They may also preserve self-cohesion by searching for compensating selfobjects; that is, they compensate for alterego failures by turning to either mirroring or idealized persons.

For example, we often read of clergy leaving their denominational home because to do less would mean compromising their beliefs that women, minorities, and the divorced should have status equal to all others in the church, that ministry and missionary work should take precedence over proselytizing and politics, that pastors have no more authority than other individuals in interpreting the Bible. Such leave-taking presents financial hardships for ministers. They lose salary, insurance, and retirement benefits as they must now serve smaller, poorer parishes in other denominations. But the emerging pain is basically emotional. "Sometimes I feel like I've left my family behind," admitted one clergywoman. "It's very sad." How do such pastors endure? Strong ideals support them in this painful relinquishment of alterego connections they have so long and lovingly forged. Values and principles they feel uplifted by, and which they have admired in others, give them the courage to face rejection and isolation. Idealized selfobjects compensate for the painful loss of alterego selfobjects.

Other ministers possess limited capacities for utilizing alternative or compensating selfobject supports. As a result they merely respond with bitterness and demoralization. It is not unusual, for instance, for young ministers to learn through experience with some parishes that they are not accepted for who they are but for what they do—not for what they do for themselves, but for others. "They made it very clear to me from the beginning," said one female pastor, "that I was there to take care of them, not them to take care of me. I really felt minimized as a person, who has needs just like theirs." Even after years of faithful service, a pastor might experience herself being accepted professionally but not personally. Deep resentment and despair about ministry may then set in. What ministers call burnout often is caused not so much by overwork as by absence of soul mates, the absence of a company of like-spirited others who sustain the heart of the pastor.

As a result of being injured by an alterego-rejecting parish, some ministers tighten the circle of their relied-upon alterego selfobjects. On the one hand, ministers may respond with alterego elitism. An example of this is clergy who claim that the only people they can really relate to are other clergy because the laity do not and cannot understand the life of the minister. This tightening of the circle not only protects the pastor's self from further injury, but can also be a form of passive aggression, an indirect expression of rage at the church for its callous behavior toward the minister.

On the other hand, clergy may fantasize about a special group to which they belong, a body of individuals who have unique and touching commonalities. A minister who grew up as the youngest child with several much older brothers never solidly experienced being like them or their being like him. He was always considered the baby, even in adult life. His struggles with alterego assurances continued in his personal and professional life. Through his therapy he came to understand how he sought to escape this chronic experience of alienation by finding identification with a vast host of individuals he called "suffering ones." Others out there had suffered as he had. They and he shared a common history. Their similar life's stories bonded them together. His decision to become a pastoral counselor was motivated in part by this core need to affiliate with and serve those who were sufferers like himself.

If alterego alienation is severe or protracted, the minister may give up efforts to establish normal connections with others altogether. The pastor may develop defensive structures to protect his self from the pain of alterego injuries. He may claim and act as though he has no real need for others, that he is basically independent. The unfortunate result is that the minister fails to respond to inviting overtures from the parish when they finally are present. He pushes aside empathic alterego responses. Eventually parishioners lose patience as they try over and over again to penetrate the pastor's defensive wall. The minister may then take their turning away as further justification for withdrawing from them. And so the boundaries build. Mirroring, idealizing, and alterego needs also shape how the pastor relates to his or her spouse, as we will see in the next several chapters.

F O U R
Pastors in
Private

ONE YOUNG LADY DATING a special fellow was being congratulated by her girlfriend. "It must be wonderful being with a guy like that," the friend bubbled. "It's not so much how he makes me feel about him when we're together that's exciting," the girl replied. "What's exciting is how he makes me feel about *me*"— a true mirroring oriented statement.

MIRRORING EXPECTATIONS

Part of the excitement of courtship is the exhilaration of two persons being mirrored by each other. A loving partner makes us feel wondrously desirable, and in the glow of that soaring state of self-esteem we respond in ways that make the other feel wondrously desirable too. At times the mutual admiration society between the pair is romantically amusing, and loving relatives will tease the couple about it. Hopefully the couple will be able to provide sustaining mirroring responses for each other long after the honeymoon is over.

Mirroring the Body

Pastors often look to their spouses for positive mirroring of the physical self. I still work hard to keep my stomach and "love handles" (sides) as flat as possible so I can elicit admiring reactions from my wife. I run and play tennis not only because they make me feel good, but also because I think they help make me look good to her. I want her to convey to me by glances and innuendos that I'm attractive, and I want her to feel drawn to me romantically, sexually. When all this happens, smoothly and with some consistency, my need for her to validate my self via my body is no big deal. Exercise and the sexual drive seem to take a normal and integrated place in the routine of my life.

But if time goes by, and by, and my spouse does not give as much energy to me as she does to the kids, her work, or her aerobics, or if she does not seem particularly interested in sex, I begin to ruminate about the situation. I usually feel mildly hurt at first, a little sad for myself and lonely, but I sensibly reason that we both have been tired and under a lot of stress. If the situation continues, however, this mild hurt turns into growing irritation. I find myself limiting my conversation to her and acting reserved. I may give subtle clues to her that I am unhappy and that she ought to notice and respond. I may very deliberately close the bedroom door for privacy before I change clothes, for example. If the situation continues and festers inside me, irritation develops into passive retaliatory thoughts. I begin to have conversations with her in my mind where I tell her off, give a long litany about her slights of me, and tell her it would probably be best for us to separate.

Far be it from me during the course of all this to say anything about how much I want her or how hurt and angry I am! That would seem weak, or would just open me up to her excuses or her tears or her complaints about my behavior. I realize even in the midst of this that I am not being helpful at all, that I am expecting her to know what is going on inside me and to make the first move toward patching things up. But my injured self feels justified in being standoffish, while my vulnerable self fears further injury if I expose my feelings.

The hurt-irritation-retaliation sequence might take different forms for others and be expressed in different ways. Moreover, the central injury in the sexual interaction might not be experienced as a failure of the spouse to meet the pastor partner's strong mirroring needs, as in my case. But the general reactions I am sharing with you—when my sexual-personal self is not mirrored in the way I want it to be or expect it to be—are common in pastors and in clergy spouses. Each of us is a body-self, and our firm self-cohesion and reliable self-esteem are established in part as we receive affirmation regarding our attractiveness, our sexual desirability, our masculinity or femininity—or, at the most basic level, as we receive validation of our gender identity (confirmation of one's self as a male or female). Although we love our partner and extend understanding and care, we still relate to the other as to a mirroring selfobject whose ministrations we rely upon if not subtly demand. Consequently, the pastor feels more or less seriously injured when these mirroring responses are experienced as absent or inadequate.

Hopefully a pastor's self-cohesion and self-esteem will not be exclusively or unduly linked with how the spouse responds to the pastor's physical self. Sometimes it is. A young clergyman who brought serious self-difficulties into his marriage expected frequent and at times bizarre sex from his wife as a means of pushing away monstrous self-doubts. Such exotic activities, and his attendant fantasies that he was an extraordinarily adept lover, momentarily infused him with the strength and confidence needed to ward off impending emotional disintegration. When he reentered the world, however, the self-doubts quickly returned, and so he reengaged his wife sexually for that passionate glue that would hold his fragmenting self together. Her protestations of "too much," or of his just "using her," were met with his angry rebuke that she really did not love him. Here was an archaic type of mirroring need, where a pastor demanded the total availability of his selfobject spouse in order to ward off the collapse of his self.

This young minister's demand for total sexual compliance from his wife was an expression of the fragmentation of his self. That is, his self-cohesion was splitting up, resulting in sexual drives running around wildly (still within the marriage, thank heaven), without these drives being integrated into an intact, firmly functioning self that set reasonable limits. It is important to realize that excessive preoccupation with sex may indicate how desperately a person is struggling to maintain self-integration. This minister's excessive sexual activity was also a floundering attempt on his part to hold his self together. However unempathic he was toward his wife, the sexual activities he demanded were remedial efforts to keep his self alive and minimally functioning in the world.

Sexual problems between clergy couples, therefore, are frequently not problems with sex per se. Sexual problems may represent the symptoms of selves who have felt injured in their hopes and expectations and are thus empty or enraged. Even physical sexual difficulties, such as diminished sexual drive, excessive sexual drive, impotency, or premature ejaculation, may be rooted in a self that is weak, vulnerable, and prone to fragmentation.

Sex often becomes the overburdened carrier by which one's self-needs are expected to be met or fixed. Sex becomes a narrow but persistent way the self seeks to be preserved, enhanced, or restored. Just like preaching, sex can become a highly sensitive occasion for the elevation of self-esteem as well as for grave self-doubts.

Mirroring the Intellect

There are other ways in which a pastor may expect the partner to function as a mirroring selfobject. Rather than the pastor's self-esteem being especially connected to physical-sexual being, the core of the pastor's self-esteem may reside in his or her intellect or creativity. Praise for a great golf swing or for a striking tan may do little for the pastor's pride, but a word of praise for his or her marvelous insights into human nature, or for the uniqueness of a sermon's verbal expression, may send secret shivers of pleasure down the pastor's spine. One female pastor requested that her husband read her sermons before she delivered them. Her purpose in that was not to gain his editorial comments but to savor the sheer joy of seeing his head nod in silent agreement and the delight in hearing him laugh at her insightful humor.

Receiving such nods and chuckles not only sustains a person, but also nourishes a deep sense of bondedness with the other. When a person receives affirming responses from the selfobject, the person is filled with a deep sense of being understood, of being firmly connected to and at one with the empathic-responding figure. This sense of connectedness to an empathically understanding and responding other is the psychological bedrock that keeps a person firm and hopeful, even as that person enters into arenas of life that challenge the person's sense of being special. These empathic responses from a selfobject-endowed spouse are also the basic blocks that keep marriages strong, even when the winds of change and stress blow against them.

We want to remember that we are attempting to understand things from the perspective of the pastor. It is from his or her internal framework that we come to know whether a partner was experienced as empathic (and thus enhancing of self-esteem) or as unempathic (and thus injuring of self-esteem). An outsider's judgment does not count. What is central is how the pastor experiences the action of the other. Thus, for example, one clergyman who prided himself on his expertise playing the viola was cut to the quick when his wife complained that he played too loudly and too long. He reprimanded her in therapy for her lack of understanding, and for "being jealous of everything that means a lot to me." I knew from his history that he had never received from his cold, detached mother the smiles and looks of approval that could have established within him the assurance of having worth. His quick mind, consequently, produced creative product after product in an effort to elicit confirmation of his worth. Even the barest hint of criticism, therefore, threw him into a rage. He needed almost perfect responses to soothe his hypersensitivity.

There was no way his wife could meet this need, any more than a parent can provide continuously perfect responses to keep a child free from tension (the child who then responds with anger or tears when his omnipotent selfobject parents fail him). I could empathize with the pastor. I recognized the meaning and importance of his over-whelming demand for noncritical, positive-energy reactions to what he said and did. But I could also empathize with his burdened wife. From his perspective she was injuring him. As is the case for many pastors who are severely mirror-hungry, nothing his spouse did was either right or enough.

Mirroring Central Values

The need for mirroring is also evident in the range of ways the pastor expects the spouse to accommodate to the pastor's values and related expectations. As a common example, the minister typically expects that the spouse will understand that the minister must spend many evenings at church meetings and many weekends on church activities. Accompanying this expectation is the assumption that the spouse values parish work and is invested in helping the pastor be a success in the church. Moreover, it is assumed that the spouse will be delighted when the pastor shines in the parish and denomination, for this will enhance not only the prestige of the minister but will benefit the life of the spouse as well.

The spouse may, indeed, resonate with the pastor's goals and ideals, but eventually the husband or wife may begin to complain about not seeing the pastor partner enough, or may complain about how the pastor's work is becoming more important than spouse and family. When the spouse becomes unhappy or disillusioned, whatever state of well-being the pastor has acquired becomes threatened to some degree. The smooth functioning of the self is disturbed. Typically the minister feels torn between work and family. On the one hand, the pastor may feel guilty, but on the other hand the pastor may feel angry at being put in a no-win situation. If, however, the pastor partner has the capacity to soothe her or his self, to keep anxiety in check, and to maintain empathy for the spouse (in short, retain self-cohesion), then the pastor partner is able to deal with the problem with under-standing and reason. The matter does not become a crisis, and the spouse remains a valued figure.

But if the pastor's self is vulnerable or chronically prone to frag-mentation, the demand for compliance from spouse and children may be tyrannical. The weakly structured pastor may expect near-total and perfect responsiveness. Any variation from what has been demanded by the pastor may elicit angry words, even physical reprisal. In this archaic self-state, life gets divided into good and bad, right and wrong, for me or against me. Everything about the spouse, therefore, is ex-perienced as either enhancing and reassuring or as irritating and in-jurious.

Spouses are often confused and hurt about all this. They do not realize how they are functioning as the pastor partner's selfobject. Moreover, they do not realize how the self of the pastor fluctuates so that at times the pastor's needs are more crucial than at others. The spouse may lose his or her status as a central selfobject figure for the partner. The pastor may eventually relate to the spouse dispassionately, as an object that no longer has a strong emotional bearing upon the life and well-being of the minister. In some cases, pastor partners generate new selfobject supports, experiencing other persons, or phys-ical things, as tremendously important. For example, organists, pa-rishioners, or clergy of the opposite sex may be absorbed by the pastor as needed and desired figures. In many cases they become the central mirroring selfobjects maintaining the pastor's self and enhancing the pastor's self-esteem.

IDEALIZING HOPES

The pastor whose self-in-ministry is sustained by deep bonds with inspiring figures may not have his or her self-in-marriage supported in the same celebrated way. The spouse's strengthening and calming selfobject role may not seem dramatic or significant, but it is. In an adequately functioning marriage, the soothing, uplifting responses from the spouse flow so smoothly that ministers tend to lose sight of their dependency upon them.

The pastor partner relies upon the idealized selfobject spouse in two basic ways. One is by borrowing values and courage from the spouse, who is perceived as a source of strength. The other is a more nonconscious reliance upon the soothing environment created by the empathically attuned spouse.

Borrowing from the
Idealized Spouse

To understand borrowing as a way of using the spouse as an idealized selfobject, let us consider what happens to the self of a pastor during normal transition times. When changes press in upon the minister, the cohesion of his or her self is threatened to some degree, even when events are happily anticipated. Untried new roles cause anxiety, and new, to-be-assumed identities create self-doubts. To ease that strain, ministers borrow strength or needed characteristics from idealized selfobjects.

This borrowing mechanism often occurs with seminary students prior to graduation. As they struggle to learn the role of being a minister, they imitate revered teachers. They borrow preaching style, phraseology, religious orientation, or attitudes toward the church from respected seminary figures. Such borrowings give confidence to the transitional self ("What I'm doing is OK because it is what my professor would do") as well as substance to the self ("There is something I can do as I try to find out how to be").

To stabilize the self, new pastors may also borrow consolidating attitudes and strengths from their spouses. "I'm not very good in social situations," confessed one seminary graduate. "My wife is much better than I am. I'm going to have to take some clues from her about how to get along and how to get things done." A new second-career minister, who experienced mild anxiety attacks before serving her first church, took within herself the confidence exuded by her husband: "He spoke so positively and with such reassurance that I started to feel that way myself." Another individual said, "My wife was a preacher's kid. I'm not sure what's going to happen out there, but she should have some perspectives that will be helpful to me."

Because these borrowings seem so normal and commonplace they may appear to be of minimal importance. Do not be fooled. In everyday life it is the reaching out and grabbing for a supportive hand and finding it reassuringly there—or demoralizingly gone—that determines whether we keep going or give up. Pastors reach for the spouse's hand. Many, thank heaven, feel the firm, responding grasp of a partner whose spirit and outlook, inward control, and deep common sense are there for the pastor to lean on and learn from.

If a pastor partner's self is chronically vulnerable, however, the pastor may need more than a borrowing of attitudes and orientations from the spouse. Instead, the minister may remain intact only as the idealized spouse constantly supplies those cohesion-giving strengths. An inadequate capacity for self-soothing leaves the minister dependent on constant emotional, intellectual, or spiritual transfusions from the strong spouse. That becomes the only way the pastor can keep functioning. The spouse, however, eventually becomes depleted by this tremendous burden, and in anger and frustration may say, "I feel like I have another child on my hands that I have to take care of!" The simile is not far from reality, for at the core of the adult pastor is a still struggling child-self needing the ministrations of a powerful take-charge person.

A pastor partner may even strive mightily to give to a spouse so that the spouse will be in a position to give to the pastor partner. One clergywoman described how terrified she had been as a child when her parents would fight and threaten to divorce. At a tender age she began to be the caretaker for her mother and father, serving as their confidant and mediator—all for the purpose of their staying together and acting strong so that she could feel embraced by their strength and soothed by their mutual parenting. In her marriage to a man who suffered from deep insecurities that led him to doubt his ability to stay married, she enacted the same caretaking function. She pampered and encouraged, tried to be accepting of his withdrawals, and sacrificed her integrity as she overlooked his sexual affair. In extraordinarily enervating ways she attempted to save her husband as a way of saving herself; that is, to give strength to him so that she might feel strengthened by his strength. To outside observers she already had the strength and courage to make it on her own. But strength and courage felt foreign to her. She did not want to be in the parental role; she wanted, instead, to look up to parental figures and to feel infused with their power. Subjectively she still felt like that little girl who could not endure without assimilating strength from idealized selfobjects.

Relying on Soothing Environments

A second major way in which the pastor partner relies upon the spouse as a supportive (idealized) selfobject is by depending upon the emotional and physical comfort zones generated by the spouse. More specifically, the minister may rely upon the spouse to provide an environment of reliability, predictability, and order for the calming and stabilizing of the pastor's self. These silently soothing environments typically operate outside our awareness if they are functioning adequately. This selfobject need becomes a crisis issue only when its fulfillment is disrupted in some way.

The reliability of the spouse's mood and manner offer a dependable atmosphere for the soothing and strengthening of the pastor. For instance, the pastor can risk falling apart momentarily from time to time, confident that the spouse will not become unglued by these outbursts. Furthermore, the steadiness of the spouse's personality can counteract experiences of fragmentation in the pastor's self. A calm air stills the pastor's inner qualms. Similarly, the predictable routine the spouse creates in the home is a source of constant assurance. As all else in the world seems up for grabs, the minister's stressed nerves find healing respite by entering into the comforting regularity of home life.

One minister's inclination was to come home to his wife with current war stories from Monday night council meetings. He anticipated she would meet him with a cup of coffee and a readiness to listen. That was all he needed. She did not have to offer suggestions, and he certainly did not want any criticism. Moreover, as he was struggling to keep his own rage and depletion in check, he did not want to worry about having to hold her together emotionally. He did not want her to interrupt the moment with talk about troubled kids, the latest defunct appliance, money matters, or illnesses in the family. He just wanted her to be with him in a quiet, soothing, ritual-type way that eased his disjointedness and helped set things back into perspective. As long as she functioned to provide this predictable, calming climate for his crisis-pressed self, he was able to settle down, to eventually listen to her concerns, and to return to work the next morning. Salvation comes in many forms.

Reliability and predictable routines generated by spouses are overlooked blessings. Without them the pastor may experience painful overstimulation or understimulation. Without them there is no holding environment that allows for continuity of the old and integration of the new. The controlled and optimal ambience provided by the spouse surrounds the pastor's self, contributing to a general sense of well-being and to specific relief from current crises.

Just as with reliability and predictability, being surrounded by order helps to induce a sense of firmness and manageability within the pastor. The biblical story of how the earth became cohesive as God created order out of chaos is a cosmic reflection of what persons inwardly experience: selves coalesce and stay firm as they experience others creating order around them.

One minister repeatedly complained in therapy about what a poor housekeeper his wife was, to the point where she would break into tears. The minister's selfobject needs were both general and specific. In general he required things orderly around him as a substitute for his weak capacity for maintaining internal order and direction. The first task of his day, for example, was to meticulously arrange things on his desk. In this small way, the external, controlled environment became part of his self, helping him feel internally in control. More specifically, however, he needed his wife to be orderly in their home as a comforting assurance that he was surrounded by someone who understood his condition and would give herself to the stabilization of his existence. The point is that pastors often unconsciously rely upon their spouses to provide reliability, predictability, and order. Here the spouse as a selfobject is idealized not in the sense of being publicly celebrated and esteemed, but in being looked to for the creation of an atmosphere that soothes, calms, and restores the pastor.

If reliably soothing selfobject figures were lacking in the pastor's growing-up years, the pastor continues to look for perfectly in-tune, allaying responses from the spouse. One minister related how he would become secretly enraged when his wife wasn't in rhythm with his need for a hug, a kiss, or sexual play. His frequent feeling of being "stressed out" required that she provide soothing, in-synch responses. When she failed to respond perfectly to his sexual-emotional cycles and instead imposed her own needs, he seethed inside.

In therapy, he came to see how his way of experiencing his wife was linked with his nonempathic, anxiety-prone mother, who in dev-astatingly consistent ways responded to him in terms of her own emotional state rather than his. When she was nervous, she invaded him with her mood even when he was momentarily fine, and when she was fine, she did not want to be upset by his current nervous worries. With his wife he anticipated at each moment reexperiencing the same painfully out-of-synch responses. Yet he could not soothe his own self. As a result, he basically turned away from his wife and regressively sought comfort by immersing himself in pornographic literature. There he fantasized about girls who intensely desired him and responded to his every whim.

Responding to Injuries

Spouses are limited in being available to lend attributes and to generate silently soothing environments. The reliability and order that the pastor expects are disrupted when the spouse decides to work outside the home, or develops new interests, or has a child, or becomes ill, or grows as an individual in behavior-altering ways. From the perspective of the pastor, the spouse is experienced as having deviated from the expected selfobject role, either mildly or severely, periodically or chronically, or somewhere in between these two ranges.

Every pastor experiences some uneasiness as the habitual patterns he or she has counted on are changed. If the pastor's self is firm, marked in this instance by internal capacities for self-soothing and anxiety reduction, then the minister will be able to accommodate to these changes and to integrate them nontraumatically into the core of his or her values and ideals. Furthermore, the minister will be able to respond empathically to the spouse's struggles, and thus serve as a soothing selfobject for the spouse.

If, however, the pastor partner is easily injured and upset, with diminished capacities for empathic regard, then alterations in routines and patterns are not experienced as changes but as losses. As a result, the minister may feel depleted or forlorn or may react with frustration and agitation toward the spouse.

The pastor may also withdraw from the partner. Some chronically vulnerable pastors are unable to establish trusted bonds with a spouse, sometimes because the pastor is fearful of being gravely disappointed. One minister, drowning in what he called "psychic soup," moved out of the bedroom. "I can't tolerate lying next to her. I'm so desperate for someone to hold me and take care of me that I'm overwhelmed by the desire that she do that. I'm so deathly afraid that she'll reject me that I have to move away from her." A pastor may withdraw from the spouse when needs for soothing, reassuring responses are threateningly intense.

In other cases, a pastor may withdraw from the spouse because the spouse is perceived as incapable of truly soothing the anxious minister's spirit. "I probably hurt my wife with my surgery preparations," reflected one clergyman. "I know I did. I told her that basically I wanted to be alone during the initial time in the hospital, that it was easier to marshal my own strength, to stay calm, if all I had to do was to concentrate on myself. I didn't want to tell her that her anxiety and her reactions to my actions made me uncomfortable, and that I felt better being alone than with her. She's a fine person, but I feel more like I have to take care of her than she being able to take care of me." Whether his wife actually lacked the capacity to be a calming influence for him is beside the point. He did not experience her as a person who had the soothing-strength he could lean upon. Better, thus, to be alone. Needless to say, such withdrawal is painful for a husband or wife who wants to be a supportive soul mate for the struggling pastor.

Sex as Soothing

In the light of this need for selfobject spouses to provide optimally comforting environments, we can understand more about the meaning of sex in clergy marriages. Rather than the pastor needing the spouse to provide mirroring sexual responses that enhance the pastor's self-esteem, the minister may look for sexual responses from the spouse that will be soothing and calming. This is normal, of course. God created our sexual inclinations not only for procreation, but also as a means for merging with another in peace-giving and peace-finding ways. What pastor or spouse has not needed a tender embrace or the intimacy of intercourse to ease tensions and resurrect feelings of well-being? What pastor or spouse has not needed the relief from inner deadness that the stimulating contact of sex provides? One pastor said earnestly, "Some days I'd sell my soul for a hug." Being held, being touched, can comfort us in the same essential way a mother's caress soothes a child. We never outgrow this need.

We come next to the last of the selfobject needs, namely alterego needs. These opening chapters give much attention to the self of the pastor. When we come to the self of the spouse and the self of the parish in later chapters, we will be able to move more rapidly, inasmuch as we will have developed a feel for the needs and reactions of the self. Better put, we will have deepened our empathic understanding. That, of course, is the goal of this book.

ALTEREGO YEARNINGS

The old saying claims that opposites attract. This may be true, but those who are alike tend to have longer and better marriages. Marriages where pastor and spouse share much in common are more enduring and better in quality. Clergy couples tend to bond firmly as they find in each other a familiar alterego, experiencing each other as essentially identical to themselves.

Once again, we may be made aware of the blessing of alterego connections only when we lose them. A retired minister whose wife died of Lou Gehrig's disease noted one particular heartache in the years that followed. "There are still satisfactions in my life, but the joy I used to feel in going places and seeing things has faded. And I know why. When there is no one to share it with, to be a mutually interested and thrilled companion, then beauty loses its luster. Life goes out of things." Many of us know personally what he means. It is more than just having a warm body around; it is the quiet inner assurance and enhancement of life's pleasures that come from being at one with a soul mate.

The need for alterego selfobject responses may be primary in the clergy couple. Here the pastor's self is principally sustained not by the spouse's bolstering of self-esteem, nor by the spouse's soothing ministrations, but by the spouse's sameness-of-self. When asked what place his wife had in his life, one minister touchingly replied, "She's my best friend." That friendship, of course, involved the mutual capacity for encouraging each other and for calming each other, but it was basically founded on the sense of similitude—"We share so many things in common and basically see things the same way." To understand the fuller meaning of this particular alterego bond, we would have to know what specific features this pastor saw in his wife that resonated with the nucleus of his own self.

A pastor may experience the spouse as essentially like the pastor in terms of mental predispositions ("We both are quiet, reflective people"). The connection may be through similar spiritual orientations ("We both have the love of the Lord as central in our lives"), or similar physical inclinations ("We are an exercise-and-stay-fit family"), or similar vocational visions ("My spouse is my unofficial co-pastor; we're a team"). Pastor and spouse do not need to be carbon copies of each other in order to have a strong and satisfying marriage, of course. Those with solid self-cohesion will be able to tolerate and enjoy the differences between them. But experiencing a basic shared reality with each other helps keep selves firm and creatively functioning.

Pressing Alterego Needs

For pastor partners with more intense alterego needs, the spouse may serve as a means of access to other individuals with whom the minister seeks to be connected. Some ministers marry to belong not so much to the spouse as to the spouse's family. More than one male minister has told me of developing a relationship with a girl on the basis of having found in her warm, accepting family something sorely missed in his own family. The pastor may joyfully adopt the family of his future spouse as a substitute for absent or flawed alterego relationships in his own past. In the new alterego group the pastor feels himself fitting in for the first time. In this context, however, activities with the spouse's brother(s) or father often become more enjoyable than the company of the spouse herself. Indeed, pastors in this situation report feeling more like a brother than a husband, for now both have became "children" of the family. In certain circumstances, roles can be lost as people become enmeshed in archaic alterego relationships.

The same pressing alterego hunger is often operative in ministers who seem to prefer to spend time with parishioners rather than with their spouses. The camaraderie at the church may satisfy relational needs in ways the spouse cannot. Associating with a greater number of individuals at one time may be experienced as more rewarding and more "true belonging" than solitary activities with one's marital partner. If the spouse complains that the minister is not content to stay at home, or expresses desires to just enjoy each other's company without others always being around, the minister may feel forlorn or may respond with solemn anger. The spouse, of course, experiences this as an injury to her or his own self, and may correspondingly respond with rage or withdrawal.

Chronic Alterego Needs

If the pastor lacks the conviction of being normal, of belonging, of others echoing similar thoughts and feelings, then the minister's alterego needs may be of an archaic nature. Here the spouse may be expected to respond as if a twin of the minister. The pastor's fragile self-cohesion is preserved only as the spouse is a perfect alterego. A female cleric in therapy related a symbolic memory that captured her alterego struggles while growing up. She remembered that her "neurotic mother" was the church secretary, and that as a little girl she stayed at the church while her mother worked. Often, she recalled, her mother and the senior pastor would go into his office, close the door behind them, and leave her outside alone for long periods. That was an excruciating experience for her. She acutely experienced the feeling of being left out, even in her own home, and felt that something must be wrong with her to make her so unhappy.

In her adult life, consequently, she became extremely sensitive to the slightest possibility of being left out. If her husband failed to tell her what he had done that day, or forgot to make interested inquiries into how her day had been, she accused him of being self-centered.

If he talked to one of their children at a family gathering and failed to report to her what he had said, she became angrily suspicious.

Moreover, she expected—demanded—perfect twinning of her mood and thought. When he did not respond to her unexpressed or ambiguously expressed needs, she berated him. "Why don't you know what I want? I had this fantasy that when we got married you'd be reflective and intuitive like me, that you'd share my dreams and hopes. Why should I care for you when I am hurt so badly by you?" She needed his constant and perfect resonance with her to overcome her painful inner isolation and the ravaging thought that somehow she was abnormal. She could tolerate no door between herself and others. Others had to be with her and had to convey that they were like her. Sexual involvements, consequently, became a high-tension testing ground for how well her husband could match himself to her. His frantic attempts to empty himself and take on her character and mood rarely made the grade. Her rage mixed with dejection led to serious thoughts of divorce and even to ruminations of suicide.

Another fragmentation-prone minister in therapy stated: "I want people to be what I call 'homomorphic.' That is, I want people connected to me to take the same form I do, the same form in ideas, in speech, in values. I don't want them to be different or try to mold me in their form." He had always felt alienated from others and uncertain of his own internal connectedness. "I want a relationship not for novelty or variety, nor for expanding skills or developing intimacy, but simply for continuity, for feeling like I have a 'me' inside." He could not tolerate accommodating to his wife, for then he lost his self in her personality. Similarly, he could not deeply share his feelings with her, for then she controlled his self via her knowledge of him. This pastor was not paranoid; he was an individual with a severely traumatized, vulnerable self. In order to achieve the barest sense of self sovereignty, as he called it, he required that his form be perfectly twinned by his alterego spouse.

Sex as Alterego Bonding

Sex serves many purposes. We have seen how it can become the means for meeting mirroring and idealizing needs. Sex can also be the way the pastor seeks fulfillment of alterego needs. Most frequently, physical touching and sexual intercourse are extensions of the pastor's feelings of bondedness with the spouse. Various experiences of self-sameness lead to sexual embraces and are celebrated in these bodily ways. Thus, while passion certainly may be involved, the physical embrace may be an extension of having shared good, harmonious times with the spouse, or an expression of mutuality when the partners feel especially united (such as when they have proudly observed the performance of their children). Then again, sexual involvement may be an enactment of reconciliation when misunderstandings have been worked out and the pastor partner once again feels connected to an in-tune husband or wife. Here sexual contact represents the minister's link with the spouse, rather than sex being used to create a bond.

Some sexual behavior, however, attempts to shore up an eroding alterego relationship. As a mild example, a husband may slide his arm around his wife and affectionately pat her bottom. "I don't know why, but I feel lonely for you," he says. His comment and caress are not about sexual hungers, but about feeling out of touch, about needing the assurance of feeling emotionally connected with a familiar, loving other, which a moment of physical intimacy might bring.

If, however, the pastor fears being left by the spouse, or fears feeling like an outsider in groups where being unmarried or divorced is atypical (which is often the case in parishes), then the pastor may attempt to sexualize the relationship as a means of holding on to the spouse. In such a case the pastor partner may intensify sexual activity and attempt to capture the spouse's sexual interest so that the angry or withdrawing spouse will stay—so, consequently, the threat to the pastor's self-cohesion can be averted. The panic of being alone and of once again not fitting in leads to sexual clinging.

In general, spouses often do not know they are providing a selfobject function. They are simply doing the best they can. The nature of the spouse's efforts, however, is likewise shaped by the condition of the spouse's own self-cohesion, and by the selfobject needs particular to each spouse.

F I V E
Spouses in the Narthex

T HE TRADITIONALLY EXPECTED role of clergy *wives* is clearly in the process of change. We can no longer "probably safely assume" that ministry as a "two-person career" (with wife as unpaid assistant) "is still an ideal as well as the norm."[6] For the most part, clergy wives today do not experience their self-image and self-esteem as being intimately linked to their husbands' ministry careers. Correspondingly, while expectations regarding the role of the pastor's wife vary from congregation to congregation, increasingly she is responded to as an individual who participates in parish life as a layperson rather than as the first lady of the church. Furthermore, male ministers are becoming more supportive of their wives' personal development, employment outside the home, and altered ways of worshiping and serving.

The role of clergy *husbands* in the church is also unclear. Husbands' own experiences regarding their place in the parish are nebulous.[7] In addition, the larger church's role expectations for clergy husbands remain largely undefined. Moreover, data regarding what female ministers expect from their spouses in the way of parish involvement are sparse.

Husbands and wives of ministers symbolically live in the narthex of the parish. They exist in that vestibule state of being a part of the congregation, on the one hand, but never able to fully sit down with them as a typical parishioner, on the other hand. Neither can they, nor may they want to, symbolically seat themselves next to the pastor's pulpit chair, as a recognized assistant in ministry. But neither can they fully step outside the church and act as if the church had no claim on them, or as if they had no expectations of the church.

Whether clergy spouse roles are new or old, enacted by males or females, wanted or detested, we are not at a loss when it comes to understanding the essential emotional connections between clergy spouse and the parish. The parish and the clergy spouse are each a self, and each in one way or another tends to respond to the other as its selfobject. The shape and intensity of that self-selfobject relationship may be different than in prior decades, as it is now for some clergy wives and parishes, or it may not have yet settled into recognizable psychological-cultural forms, as is the case now with clergy husbands and parishes, but the reality of the self-selfobject relating is always indelibly present. At times the parish may function only marginally as the clergy spouse's mirroring, idealized, or alterego selfobject, serving more as part of the background fabric of the spouse's daily world. At other times the relationship with the parish is more focused and central to the well-being of the spouse. At the other extreme are severe, archaic expectations, if not demands, for the parish to meet the needs of the spouse's vulnerable self. The church will always be a psychological part of clergy spouses to some degree, and thus the spouses will have some expectation that the parish will function in mirroring, idealized, or alterego ways.

Some examples in this chapter will reflect the longer, ongoing relationship between clergy wives and the church, while some will touch on clergy husbands. The same self dynamics apply to all, and to new as well as old types of interaction.

MIRRORING NEEDS

Clergy spouses normally enjoy being appreciated and admired by others. At the very least, they hope that parishioners will like them, will like their children, and will like their pastor partner. Some spouses are concerned with making a good impression through their housekeeping and child-rearing activities. Others find satisfaction in being respected for their thoughtfulness, or intellect, or professional career work. At times a clergy husband may try to make sure that parishioners know he is a good provider, wanting them to clearly understand that his wife is working in the church because she wants to rather than needs to. Even if the church is not central to the identity or self-esteem of certain spouses, they typically remain somewhat sensitive to how parishioners picture them if not talk about them. This sensitivity is not paranoia or excessive self-consciousness. It is an example of how the selves of clergy spouses are normally attuned to the presence or absence of affirming responses from the church. As stated previously, at times the clergy spouse habitually relies upon validating responses as part of the background fabric of life. The validations only come into active consciousness when they are absent or change in some disturbing way.

At other times the clergy spouse actively seeks mirroring responses. For some clergy wives, the prestige they enjoy comes fundamentally from being "the pastor's wife," and they play this role to the hilt. These insufficiently modified needs for mirroring acclaim, however, should not blind us to the very real and healthy contributions to the clergy wife's self-esteem that can come through being viewed as special via her role as the pastor's spouse.

But clergy wives have needs for direct mirroring rather than just deflected mirroring. They want to be admired for what they do themselves, not just for their role as the pastor's mate. About 80 percent of ministers grew up as an oldest child. About half of ministers' wives did so as well, and they are likely to be competitive with their husbands in finding ways of helping and serving for which they will be appreciated and admired.[8]

Needs of clergy wives for direct affirmation are strong. This has probably always been true to some extent. If it is accurate to say (and I think it is) that the ministry of the church has been carried along in goodly measure through the efforts of clergy wives, then we are bound to find a fair number of confident, resourceful, proud women whose desires for recognition and applause have been as intense as any male minister's. Indeed, the admiration they receive or look for often sustains them in their efforts. A lot of work gets done in the church through ego, and not only the male's.

Pressing Mirroring Needs

Pressing mirroring needs of a clergy spouse may not be recognized when the spouse seeks fulfillment of these needs via other routes. For example, a clergy wife in therapy came to the point where she could genuinely say, "I feel softer, more caring than I've ever been. And yet I still have these desperate needs to compete and be special. Maybe I can be special by being an outstanding care-giver in the church." Wishes to shine and be outstanding are often wrapped in care-providing endeavors, giving the impression that the individual is devoid of motives for excelling over others and being publicly acclaimed. Such, however, is not always the case.

Some clergy spouses operate out of a grandiose self that automatically expects the parish to respond as a mirroring selfobject. They may, for example, confront the church with their position and expect the church to comply. One husband simply rebelled against any suggestion that he involve himself in the congregation where his pastor partner served. That was her work, not his. When he did attend church, he was standoffish, at times actually rude. "From the first time I meet parishioners with my wife, I tell them what I'm going to do, and how I'm going to be in church, and that takes care of that." This orientation originated not so much from an underlying anxiety that the parish would attempt to consume his life—as was the fear for another clergy husband—but more from an attitude of expecting perfect compliance from others. He expected the parish to respond as an accommodating selfobject that simply molded itself to his wishes. He was like a child who implicitly expects that those around him will automatically grant his demands to do whatever he wants.

Other clergy spouses operate from a chronically vulnerable self. Dependent upon constant affirmation from others for assured self-esteem, these individuals not only knock themselves out trying to be what they think the parish expects them to be, but they knock themselves out trying to live up to their own anxiety-driven, unrealistic expectations. They strive to receive the love and goodwill of the parish by being super-spouse, super-parent, and super-church partner. As with most severely uncertain selves, no amount of excellent effort or public reassurance convinces them they have made the grade and can now relax. Each occasion and each day involves the effort to legitimize their individual existences.

Injuries to the Spouse

The mirroring needs of clergy spouses are inevitably thwarted at times by the parish. Some are minor injuries that the spouse can intellectually understand and accept. Others are moderate injuries that the spouse can forgive. Others are severe injuries that leave the spouse devastated. All cases bring some degree of depletion or rage.

Not infrequently the praise a parish extends is frustrating rather than fortifying. Parishioners tend to make such statements as, "If this [misfortune] had to happen, it's good it happened to you because you can handle it"; as though somehow the spouse is stronger and should be able to handle pain and crises, as though the spouse has a direct pipeline to God that assures him or her of always being able to bear up. This still happens to my wife, who twenty-three years ago gave birth to our handicapped daughter. The "you-can-handle-it" praise is not only empty, it infuriates, for there is little recognition in it of the continuing struggle, and limited appreciation for the fact that one continues not with a sense of pride in what one is doing, but simply because one must. The lingering aura that the minister's family is especially strong and religiously self-sufficient is not only hollow but also isolating, for parishioners then fail to empathically meet the needs of the pastor's family.

At other times there is a diminution of the spouse's value, along with subtle allusions to the spouse's potentially negative impact. One depressed pastor's wife said she was afraid to talk in groups or express opinions because it would be taken as what the pastor felt. The blow to her self-esteem was twofold. First, she had gathered the message that her comments and actions in the parish could hurt her husband, but that nothing she did could really enhance his position. In short, she was not to be admired for her strengths and positive contributions but rather was deemed "a good pastor's wife" by not rocking the boat. Second, and closely linked, she was not being heard and received for herself as a person, but only as an extension of her husband—and a potentially dangerous one at that. Her already vulnerable self tended to retreat even further behind cautious comments and superficial conversation.

A more assertive clergy wife felt highly insulted when parishioners would give her messages to relay to the minister because "We don't want to disturb him"; as though she were simply an answering machine who was not too important to disturb. Moreover, she became enraged when church members acted as if she knew everything that was going on in the church and should have answers regarding its programs and policies. "They would not even think of coming up to my husband and asking him how to write a life insurance policy just because I sell insurance. But they come up to me expecting that I'll know about major decisions going on in the church and how they'll be handled. It infuriates me!" Each clergy spouse has some story that could be told here.

IDEALIZING NEEDS

We all need persons and groups to look up to, to be inspired by, whose presence comforts us and whose values strengthen us. Many of us have come to regard the church as a special place and force in our lives, whose arms are ready to lovingly embrace us, and whose call to higher purposes impels us toward our best self. That proclivity to respond to the church as an idealized selfobject may be even more likely for a clergy spouse, who may wed personal regard for the church with the pastor partner's dedicated commitment to it. Quite normally, a spouse may experience the parish as an intimate part of his or her inner world, and more or less rely on the parish's continued specialness as a stabilizing factor in life.

Types of Idealization

The clergy spouse may idealize the parish in a wide range of ways. An aura may surround the church as the spouse is touched by this awesome *holy place,* whose walls and windows, litanies and prayers reverberate with the mysterious presence of the divine. Then again, the idealization may focus more on the parish as a *community of believers,* whose worshiping faith joins with and marvelously magnifies the spouse's own religious assurances. The idealization may center primarily on the parish as a *healing community,* whose empathic care consoles the spouse's aching, lonely heart. Or, again, the idealization of the church may be linked to the *personality of the parish folk*—their openness, friendliness, level-headed thinking—which helps to solidify and firmly ground the spouse's mental and emotional reactions. Finally, the church may be idealized as that *community providing for the needs of and showing respect toward the pastor and the pastor's family.* The intensity of these idealizations may vary in each instance, but the point is that every clergy spouse who appropriates the parish as an idealized selfobject does so in terms of his or her own particular inner experiences and expectations.

Pressing Idealization Needs

For some spouses, the parish is a wonderful support while they are going through personal crises. One man, whose wife died during her ministry, said, "I don't see how anyone going through something like this can get along without the church. It's my lifeline. Without it I'd drown." While his warm feelings of gratitude were for specific persons in the church who comforted him, they were also for that gathered community as a whole. That specific church, and the church at large, became ever more envisioned as a source of love and sustaining good-will.

When crises threaten to undo a spouse's hold on his or her self, the spouse may cling to the church and its message in a regressive, magical way. For instance, a middle-aged woman's world began to fall apart when her pastor partner decided to divorce her. Neither her pleading nor promises could move him to continue their relationship, upon which she was very dependent. In a desperate effort to maintain her self-cohesion by preserving the cherished image that he would always be with her, she latched on to the zealous proclamations of a fundamentalist group and its evangelist. She ingested their dictates that while civil and religious institutions might annul marriages, God never does. Because God's name is invoked at wedding services, the group held, marriage is a bond that can never be broken. The woman's fragmenting self found something to hold on to in this belief that under the laws of God her husband could never leave her. The specific message that spoke to her situation, combined with the comforting strength with which it was asserted, led her to join the fundamentalist group and to echo its theological and moral lessons.

Other clergy spouses exhibit archaic idealizations of the church. They may claim that the church is infallible, or that the only road to salvation lies in believing as their church believes, or that their church's way of proving one is a "true believer" is the premier if not only way. For certain spouses, this rigid and obsessive elevation of the church is a passing phenomenon, a way station toward mature religious development, analogous to the excesses of adolescence on the way to balanced integration.

But certain spouses are chronically fixated at this archaic stage of idealization. Pathological idealization of the church can arise as an emotionally vulnerable individual relinquishes his or her self to a religious group offering the certainty of power and truth. One clergy spouse became so absorbed in a church and its teachings that he treated his own children in accordance with prescribed dogma rather than in terms of their emotional needs. "Spare the rod and spoil the child," an Old Testament proverb made the basis of a child-discipline approach, came close to child abuse in this case. The parish and its teachings were rigid ideals that functioned in life-limiting and threatening ways.

Experienced Injuries

Healthy, mature idealization of the parish does not deny that the church is human and imperfect. Idealism without realism becomes sentimentality. On the other hand, realism without idealism becomes cynicism.[9] The ability of the clergy spouse to hold the church in high esteem even in difficult times protects the spouse from sliding into despair regarding the church.

That does not mean that clergy spouses do not become intensely upset with the parish, especially when it fails to fulfill its perceived mission. When some 200 clergy wives were asked to write anonymous letters expressing what they would like to say to their congregations if there were no fear of reprisal, one of the major concerns they expressed was about congregations' "lacking a sense of urgent purpose."[10] Clergy spouses often experience a disturbing gap between what they envision for the church and the reality they actually encounter.

At times a clergy spouse's criticisms are loving agonies, expressed hurts that try to prompt the church to be what the spouse knows it can be. "My disappointment in our congregation," confided one husband, "is that it has lost the vision of its specialness and is no longer led by the power of its own commitments." Then again, some judgments from spouses come as frustrated slaps at the church: "Don't expect me to come to the women's guild when you have a program on hunger and then vote to spend our treasury money on a fancy women's luncheon."

Clergy spouses feel injured when the supposedly empathic parish acts with insensitivity toward the needs of the pastor's family. Said one, "I wish the church would understand that my working outside and inside the home allows me little time to be as involved as it would like me to be in parish activities. And I wish the congregation would realize that we need 'the pastor' as much here at home as they do at church. But they don't seem to. I used to be excited and positive about ministry. Now I feel like the negative minister's spouse I once never understood."

Disillusionment may become so powerful that the spouse comes to despise the church once dearly cherished and leaned upon. When one pastor was summarily fired after twenty-three years of faithful service, his wife was so embittered that she could no longer set foot in any church. Not just the future but also the past became blackened: "Now I see that all that love and friendship shown to us through the years were just lies. None of it was true." Participation in church life is central to the spiritual and emotional well-being of many clergy spouses. Inevitably, to some degree, that very church becomes a source of pain and stress, disrupting inner tranquility and threatening the spouse's values.

Finally, some clergy spouses have little or no attachment to the church at all, perhaps because of a commitment to secular humanism, atheistic beliefs, or another faith. Or nonattachment may be the result of the spouse's having been overwhelmingly injured by the church in the past.

Another, often unrecognized, reason for this lack of attachment is failure to share the parish's idealization of the pastor. Typically, idealization of a parish is based upon idealization of the minister, just like high regard for a group is often based upon admiration for its leader, or nostalgic images of family life are rooted in hallowed remembrances of mom and dad. An old saying quips, however, that a man can be a hero to everyone but his valet. Unfortunately, pastors can often be heroes to everyone but their spouses. It is difficult for someone to feel spiritually fed by a pastor when the pastor is that person's marriage partner—whom the spouse sees physically, emotionally, and morally naked as no one else does. "Sermons are just my husband talking," said one wife. "I feel cheated in my own spiritual life, for I don't have a pastor who I can turn to and feel inspired by." The spouse may lack a sense of oneness with parishioners who are bonded together through their idealizing respect for the minister. As a consequence, the parish may lack that aura of specialness for the spouse.

ALTEREGO NEEDS

We recall that an alterego relationship is an experience of sameness and the sense of acceptance. The presence of others who are like us in crucial ways contributes to our sense of belonging, of having normal thoughts, beliefs, skills, and behaviors, and of living in a human environment. Geographical places, things, and familiar life practices can also function as alterego supports, as objects we experience as extensions of our nature, tastes, and habits, that reflect who we are and preserve our personal history. When we feel down or lonely, or miss our families and become nostalgic about our home church and past experiences, all of us try to pull around us the comfort of familiar alterego persons and objects. We may take out old pictures, or hum old hymns we grew up on, or call a friend whose voice confirms our reality. Momentarily reimmersed in those bonds, we surface again, grasping life with a fuller embrace.

The wife of a pastor wrote me an urgent message after hearing that I was working on a book about clergy marriages. "In your book, Dr. Randall, please, *please* consider second career ministry families separately. My husband and I have been married 18 years, and have just survived (I think) our first year as a clergy couple. We find that out in the 'real world' we are isolated not only from nonclergy people, but also from other first career clergy couples. We simply don't have that much in common besides my husband's work, and that's the last thing we need to talk about in social situations."

Her letter is heart-wrenching. Although her situation merits special attention, it points up the fact that central to the selves of some clergy spouses is the need to be surrounded by others who share a life similar to their own, whose presence makes them feel they are not alone.

Wide Range of Comfort Zones

People vary, of course, in the range of their alterego comfort zones. Some clergy spouses feel at home in almost any circumstance. "People are people, and we're all God's children," intoned one missionary wife, who seemed able to relate intimately to individuals of vastly different cultures. For her, cultural and racial similarities were not those features she needed to sense connectedness and belonging. Nursing mothers concerned with their babies were just like her, and people who wanted to better their living conditions fit in with her own goals of self-help. The traits of others she needed around her to feel in a human environment were wide indeed. Beyond the strangeness of custom or physical appearance, she could fathom a universal humanness, a community of divinely created souls, with which she could resonate. In a healthy way, she opened herself to the world, and connected with it.

This capacity to perceive affinities between oneself and others allows some missionary spouses to work productively in circumstances others would experience as depressingly alien. These missionary spouses are probably sustained as well by the memory of strong bonds with same-self souls back home. Supportive alterego persons become portable as we carry them in our mind from place to place.

These missionary spouses may be nourished also as familiar patterns are re-created in the foreign milieu—for example, as they demonstrate skills to others and then see the skills practiced, or teach about Jesus and then hear the old familiar stories related back, or coach native children in the play of fondly remembered games. In all these ways an atmosphere of familiarity to their origins is reestablished, giving a reassuring continuity and a grounding to life.

Typical Alterego Expectations

Most clergy spouses (like most individuals) fall in the middle range of alterego needs and expectations. When clergy spouses move into new parish communities, their emotional radar system automatically clicks on. They scan faces and voices, schools and shopping centers, lawns and houses for some assurance that they are in a comfortable environment. They monitor the parish, instinctively assessing whether practices are sufficiently familiar so they can feel at home, or whether parishioners seem enough like themselves so they can "be themselves." This is not egotism or bigotry. It is the normal need of the self for the companionship of kindred spirits and for an ambience of comforting familiarity. The spouse may joyfully anticipate the adventure of meeting unique individuals and learning more about life from them. This remains an adventure rather than an ordeal as long as there is a secure home base of alterego persons to whom the spouse can return—physically or in memory.

A clergy spouse may also hope that the parish will be a place where he or she can overcome previous feelings of alienation or being different. One clergy husband in his forties expressed the pain of a dual estrangement. "Somehow when I'm with people, I feel on the fringe, not really part of them. That's especially true when the men gather in a corner. When they talk I feel like I did when I was a kid listening to my dad and his friends talk, just there and not grown up." But on a men's church retreat he reported the delightful experience of "feeling like a man, not a boy." His account hinted at a kind of locker-room camaraderie, a confirming experience of being part of the gang. The experience was also something of a passage into manhood, as mature-acting men responded as if he were like them and they were like him. It is common for clergy spouses to look to the church for those selfobject experiences they missed early in life. In the parish the spouse may seek a substitute for the empathic responses he or she needs.

If the cohesion of the clergy spouse is firmly formed, he or she can establish personally satisfying relationships with a variety of persons. Near-perfect correspondence between self and others does not become a prerequisite for bonding. Moreover, when alterego relationships are absent in the parish, the self-secure spouse has the capacity to search elsewhere for a like-minded group. If relationships are disappointing, the spouse has the ability to retain self-cohesion by turning to the mirroring affirmations of others, or to the comforting strength of others (the ability to use compensating selfobject responses). No matter how firm the spouse's self is, however, there are always some hurts and frustrations when one feels cut off from kindred spirits.

Disappointing Alterego Relations

The availability of alterego figures and the problem of loneliness in the parish are intimately related. Loneliness is often a central issue for clergy spouses in the parish. Mace and Mace found that 48 percent of pastors' wives listed a lack of in-depth sharing with other couples as a decided disadvantage of clergy marriage.[11] Pat Valeriano's 1981 survey of 166 ministers' wives found that loneliness is a central result of ministry.[12] Marilyn Brown Oden's 1988 analysis of 200 anonymous letters from clergy spouses, sent to her at her request, revealed loneliness as a predominant concern.[13]

Loneliness in the parish arises primarily because alterego relationships are unavailable or disappointing. Within the church, clergy spouses have many acquaintances with whom they are cordial, but a large proportion of clergy wives apparently have no real parish soul mates with whom they can dare to bare all their flaws and still feel accepted.

The spouse may experience a lack of sameness-of-self with the parish on the most basic of levels. A young minister's wife found herself lonely in a church made up mostly of old women. The relationship was cordial with these ladies, but the wife longed for persons her own age with whom she could relate, whose children were closer to hers in age, and whose life concerns were similar. Correspondingly, a city-raised, streetwise husband found himself trying to relate to the conservative, Corn Belt farmers who belonged to a rural church served by his wife. Once again, the relationship was civil, but both sides felt a disjuncture between them. Good old homesickness often arises not so much from having left persons behind as from being unable to find adequate substitutes for them in the present place.

Physical age or cultural origins are not the only conditions that can automatically bond persons, of course. Particular life circumstances may cause a spouse to look for specific alterego relationships within the parish. Another young clergy wife was surrounded by young parish mothers like herself, and yet she still felt different. She sensed herself in a different state of life, even at a different level of maturity, for unlike them she had already lost both of her beloved parents. She had nursed them physically and emotionally, had buried them, and had worked through a traumatic adjustment usually reserved for a person much older. The complaints and worries of the parish women her own age seemed trivial. The more she heard them, the more annoyed she became. Older women, who had already lost their parents, were also different from her. She longed to find people like herself who had similar experiences, but she despaired of doing so. "I don't know anyone who has gone through what I have at my age. People in this church are nice, but there's nobody who I can really connect with, who could sense without me trying to explain it all what I feel. It seems strange to say, but because of that I don't feel like I fit in."

Loneliness also arises when parish members remain distant. One clergy wife, who lived in a small town and was not employed, found that the parishioners were neighborly but none tried to become close friends. One woman in the congregation always asked the pastor's wife how she was and expressed missing her when she was not at worship. That woman, like the others, never invited her to her home, however. One evening the pastor's wife encouraged the woman to come over for a quiet cup of tea. She accepted with some reluctance. Finally the woman frankly stated that she could not be close friends with the pastor's wife because that might offend other people in the parish. In fact, she added, most people in the church felt the same way. "I was very hurt," the wife expressed later. "It makes me hesitant to try to be close to any other woman in the church. I don't want to be put down again."

Such putdowns are often felt as rejection, as giving the message, "We don't want to be a part of you because you're different, and if we tried it would cause us trouble." The assumed "difference" may perplex and infuriate the clergy spouse, who wants to scream back, "Just because I'm married to the pastor does not mean I'm more spiritual than anyone else, or more straitlaced, or more self-sufficient, or will betray confidences to the pastor. Despite your preconceptions, a minister's spouse is human!"

We will not discuss here the disastrous experiences that result from clergy spouses having *their* confidences betrayed by close parish friendships. No matter how well established the spouse's self-esteem may be, such breaches of confidence are always devastating. They are friendship's form of infidelity.

Reactions to Alterego Disappointments

Some clergy spouses mask their loneliness. They act graciously, they show concern, they relate pleasantly, but at their center they are depressingly empty. Their highly adaptive behavior may win the respect and admiration of others, but that does not fill the void. For them, their hidden longing is not for the prize of social praise, but for the peace of feeling intimately connected.

Some of the difficulty may rest in the clergy spouse's fear of being further alienated. Said one, "Sometimes I find it difficult not to form friendships, especially when certain parishioners tend to get closer to you than others do and you seem to relate to them better. But I know too many instances where close friendships in the parish caused much jealousy and resentment, and so I often turn down invitations to go out for fear of alienating others in the church." This is not always a magnanimous gesture on a clergy spouse's part; it is often a defense against being personally resented and publicly shunned, in even superficial ways. If a spouse lacks confidence in making friends, or in dealing with others' reactions, then forming only cordial acquaintanceships in the parish becomes a defensive move, even though the yearning for deeper bonds goes unfulfilled.

Indeed, apprehension of suffering the embarrassment of rejection has led some clergy spouses to translate personal worries into pastoral policies. Clergy spouses may say that it is wrong to single out friends in the parish because others would feel slighted or hurt. Here an ethical directive relieves the spouse of troublesome decisions when parishioners stimulate those yearnings for special friendship intimacies. Such a policy may cover up the spouse's fear of being unable to make friends, or the fear of being rejected once a close friendship is formed.

Archaic Alterego Needs

A clergy spouse may be able to relate to only a narrow range of individuals. The spouse may be capable of working and worshiping comfortably only with persons of the same nationality, same religious background, same educational experience, or some other characteristic central to the spouse's identity.

Even more chronically dependent upon narrowly defined alterego figures are spouses who can relate only to family members, or can sustain friendships only with persons they have known since childhood days. Meeting new parishioners or entering into a group at church creates tremendous anxiety, translated into such symptoms as headaches, colitis, and general weakness. One clergy wife stayed in the kitchen during most of the coffee hour between services and had to leave the worship service soon after it started. Contact-shunning spouses often suffer from the inability to experience others as their alterego selfobjects, as persons sufficiently like them with whom they can feel safely connected.

Clergy spouses long to feel whole and secure. As they enter a parish, their hopes for belonging and for intimacy are stimulated. At the same time, all the self-difficulties and history of previous injuries become mobilized as well. Opportunities arise for restoration of the self, on the one hand, while potent possibilities exist for reinjured self-esteem, fragmentation, and the rise of despondency or rage on the other. These hopes and dangers also exist in the relationship with the pastor partner, as we will see in the next chapter.

S I X
Spouses in Private

A WOMAN IN HER EARLY thirties married a successful middle-aged minister. This was the second marriage for both, she having divorced her husband and he having been widowed for two years. The new bride was basically a self-assured business-woman who excelled in her career and handled her finances well. Although she had wrestled with periods of low self-esteem, she generally felt good about herself.

After several months of marriage she began to feel anxious and unhappy. Although she continued her career full-time, she started to worry about her role as the minister's wife. She was not sure that she was fitting into the church properly and was not sure what her husband expected of her when they attended church functions together. She felt herself trying hard to measure up, but was frustrated at not knowing what the goals were or how to evaluate her performance. Her thoughts began to be occupied by what other people in the church might be thinking about her.

She also felt increasingly alienated from her husband. While in their courting and early honeymoon days he had treated her as the love of his life, she discovered that he had another love she had not suspected: the church. Not only the amount of time spent with parishioners but also the quality of pleasure it seemed to give him made her feel inadequate as a person and as a wife. She began to doubt her intellectual and physical attractiveness, and worried that she was not lovable.

Whenever she tried to convey to him how his actions and moods affected her, he became defensive. First he would ask when or how he had shown lack of attention to her. When she tried to tell him, he irritably replied, "It's all in your head." This response both antagonized her and panicked her, for she needed to feel that someone really did understand her, really could validate her experiences. In an intensified effort to get him to finally understand her, she became more vocally and physically animated. This only led him to explode that she was "paranoid" and "mentally ill."

MIRRORING EXPECTATIONS

Clergy spouses need attuned mirroring of their selves from the marriage partner. They need affirmative responses that keep their selves strong. Without it in certain circumstances, spouses can become fragmented, as was happening to this particular woman. For some spouses the need is more for supportive mirroring of their identity. Other spouses require empathic mirroring that nurtures their self-esteem. Still others yearn for resonant mirroring that validates their subjective truth. This woman needed all three from her pastor partner.

Mirroring Identity

A line from a powerful old hymn sings out that "new occasions teach new duties." They also require new or altered identities. The clergy spouse often confronts new occasions that call for the forging of new self-images and sometimes for the relinquishing of old ones. Such a process always involves anxiety. Affirming responses from others help sustain our confidence as we go through such stretching changes.

The clergy spouse in the above example did not need her husband's support for the development of a core of identity. Unlike some clergy spouses who have no firm sense of who they are, this woman possessed healthy self-identity. Moreover, she did not need her husband's support in order to establish a separate identity. Unlike some clergy spouses whose identity is merged with the personality of a powerful figure in their lives, she clearly possessed the conviction of her own talents, values, and beliefs. What she was struggling to establish, instead, was an appropriate identity for a certain situation, a fitting identity that would ease her performance anxiety and assure her that she was being a contributing helpmate to her husband.

His routine response to her that she could "do whatever she wanted," or that she was "doing all right," did not help her. She was not looking for permission to be herself, nor was she looking for a general pat on the back. That type of response felt patronizing. Instead, she turned to him to confirm specific things she did, for the joy and satisfaction of knowing that her practiced efforts were fitting and responsible and mattered to him and his ministry. In the inevitable stress of this transition period, she needed him to buttress her attempts at enacting a new identity by emotionally reinforcing her specific actions and attitudes.

This is but one example among many of how new identities need affirming responses. Developing the self-image of being a worker outside the home; attempting to expand one's self by joining a new group; trying to adjust one's self-picture after a promotion, graduation, birth of a child, or successful weight-loss program; or learning to live with the vision of oneself as a working parent whose children are left in the care of others; or struggling with what it means to be a retiree at the very time that one's spouse begins excited full-time work in the church—all these pressures for establishing altered identities shake the cohesion of the self. At these times, situation-specific affirming responses from the pastor partner are sorely needed: sensible applauding of efforts toward self-development; validating new tasks and responsibilities as significant contributions; appropriately praising the courage to risk failure and to risk the changes of success. When spouses feel empathically supported in these ways, transitions are made nontraumatically, and the marital bond stays firm.

Clergy spouses, however, experience injuries to their selves when their partners' responses are inadequate or unempathic. The minister may expect the spouse to work out the new identity alone, or may convey the attitude that the spouse's concerns are "no big deal." If the pastor, believing that the spouse's central role is to echo the pastor's self, secretly fears the change the spouse is going through in trying to establish a separate identity, the pastor may undercut the spouse's efforts to forge an expanded identity. Thus when the spouse tries to express his or her self in ways that do not fit into the pastor's way of seeing and understanding, the pastor may attack or criticize the spouse. Ignoring the spouse or withholding praise may also be expressions of the pastor's rage. The spouse is left feeling inadequate and impaired and may attempt to regain some semblance of self-certainty by trying to fit into the pastor partner's image of what the spouse should be.

Mirroring Esteem

A clergy spouse may not need mirroring responses that affirm a new identity. Instead, the spouse may look to the partner to bolster self-esteem. When the spouse's self-esteem begins to weaken, with the rise of disturbing doubts and misgivings, he or she may rely more intensely upon mirroring responses for the fortification of self-esteem.

The clergy wife in our example looked for reassurances that she was still special and dear to her new husband. More specifically, she needed reassurance that he still found her intellectually stimulating as well as physically attractive. Anxiety about this arose from several sources. First, as her husband resumed a full work schedule, the time and energy patterns of their courtship relationship were suddenly disrupted. Second, she experienced him turning from her to something that seemed more delightful and satisfying, namely the church. Finally, the new intimacy of the marriage called forth old memories of being hurt and abandoned. She had anticipated that his attentive manner with her would keep her feeling good about herself and would help her overcome self-doubts generated in childhood and in her first marriage. When her supersensitivity to injury at this time encountered his obsessive work habits and need for his own mirroring acclaim, the core of her self-esteem was threatened.

She felt that he was merely trying to placate her with his retorts that he still loved her and found her attractive. In her uncertain state she yearned for him to linger with her, to really see her and hear her, to show genuine interest in what she was reading, and to use her as a confidant and sounding board for problems in the church. She was experiencing in part what other clergy spouses have often felt, namely the deflation when the pastor partner seems to turn to others as more important, or turns away from ideas the spouse feels could be helpful in the human interactions of ministry. The absence of concrete mirroring responses from the pastor partner can erode a spouse's sense of worth and competency.

Clergy spouses often wish their partners would give them the same attentiveness they give to parishioners. The lack of thoughtful support for the spouse's self-esteem may come as the minister operates out of a ministry-to-pain orientation. "My first and primary obligation," said one pastor, "is to those in pain." For his family this meant that if they were not in pain, or not in as much pain as others the pastor worked with, he expected them to get by on their own. Other ministers work from an I'll-tell-you-if-anything's-wrong orientation. Here the spouse is told not to expect compliments and praise, but to realize that everything is fine unless the pastor partner says that something is wrong. Both of these approaches are reactive in nature; that is, affirmation of the other is given only when a certain level of crisis is reached. Neither of these approaches is protective, attentive to the normal needs for affirmation at all times. Many otherwise caring pastors know better than this, but unfortunately they lapse into a neglecting stupor when they enter the parsonage door. As the pastoral role is dropped, so sometimes is the personal care.

Finally, the spouse may be reluctant to ask for the self-esteem boosts he or she yearns for from the pastor partner. Remember Mr. Charles Talbot, whom we met in our opening pages? He wanted so much for his wife to tell him how great he looked and to show him she wanted to be with him. When she failed to do so, he withdrew angrily within himself. "It would have been too humiliating to ask her for that kind of attention," he later admitted. "It would have seemed like begging, especially after she didn't give it voluntarily. I couldn't let myself be vulnerable by telling her what I wanted her to do." Blows to spouses' self-esteem come not only from unempathic selfobject partners, but also from internal feelings of shame.

Mirroring Subjective Truth

What may be most crucial for a clergy spouse is the validation of his or her subjective truth. In order to enjoy a firm sense of self-assuredness down deep in our bones, we must possess a firm belief in the validity of our subjective experiences; that is, we must have confidence in our perceptions, our emotional reactions, and in the meaning we find in events that happen to us. This firm belief in our values builds as significant figures in our life validate our subjective experiences, confirming them as real, right, and relevant.

When such validating responses are absent, or when others try to undermine the felt truth of our experiences, our hold on our subjective reality becomes unsteady and the core of our self is threatened with disintegration. In this tremendously anxious state, we look desperately for mirroring responses that will validate our experiences and thus help us hold our self together. Should we fail to get others to validate the truth of our experiences, we become even more anxious and thus try all the harder to make others understand what we feel. Sometimes we become loud and angry, or hysterical, or act in bizarre ways in an effort to convey the truth of how things are for us. These excessive attempts are not symptoms of craziness; they are desperate efforts to ward off the disintegration of our self by getting others to affirm the reality and meaning of our inner experiences.

The clergy spouse in our example needed her husband to validate the truth of her subjective experiences. She needed him to understand her hurt, to attune himself to the felt rightness of her upset reactions so that she could regain a sense of well-being. At first she did not need him to confess his shortcomings, but only to acknowledge that her feelings of loneliness were genuine. When he defensively attempted to insert reality into the situation by asking for an itemized list of when and how he had neglected her, she felt more injured, angry, and isolated. She struck back with more accusations and with attempts to get him to acknowledge his role. His escalating statements that it was "all in her head" threatened her emotional hold even more. In her outrage mixed with panic, she intensified her efforts to break through to him: she hit him with pillows, and told others of his grossly inconsiderate behavior. His reply that she was mentally ill only contributed to the threatened dissolution of her psyche as her subjective experiences were once again denied a hearing.

A clergy spouse's self-cohesion remains firm via mirroring support for his or her subjective truth. That subjective truth may be a wife's intuition that something is seriously troubling a son or daughter, or it may be a husband's perception that his pastor partner is being used by the senior minister, or it may be a spouse's contention that a member of the opposite sex is acting in a flirtatious way with the pastor. If the self of the clergy spouse is firm, he or she will not need total agreement with that intuition, perception, or contention, but will feel affirmed as the pastor partner listens appreciatively, attempts to understand, and takes the subjective experiences under due consideration. The more fragile the self of the spouse is, however, the more he or she insists that these experiences be validated, accepted, and acted upon. In all cases, there is some reality to what the spouse is experiencing, even if the form in which it is expressed is of a hysterical or paranoid nature. Indeed, as we have suggested, extreme forms of thinking and acting may be desperate attempts to finally awaken the selfobject world to the felt truth of what the clergy spouse is living.

IDEALIZING HOPES

In the book of Proverbs we read words like these: "A wife of noble character . . . is worth far more than rubies. . . . Her children arise and call her blessed; her husband also, and he praises her" (31:10, 28).

The images may be antiquated but the sentiment is timeless—and genderless. What a precious experience it is to have a husband or wife one can respect, trust, and rely on. We look for partners who can understand us when we talk, and who remain calm when we tell them of difficulties. We yearn for a spouse who can speak words of guidance, who can handle things pragmatically and emotionally, who is able to resonate with us but not become upset when we are depressed or irritable. What a blessing to be joined with one whose firm and faith-filled spirit can soothe our worry-riddled mind. The overarching psychological concept that points to the breadth and complexity of this reassuring link with others we deem as special is that of connectedness with idealized selfobjects.

Many clergy spouses healthily lean upon a strong, calming marriage partner for the maintenance of their own self-cohesion. At times the pastor partner serves as an idealized selfobject through personal charisma. Then again, a spouse may initially (and ongoingly) be attracted to the partner due to his or her idealized role as pastor. Most commonly, the personal strengths and the expected strengths of the pastor partner merge indistinguishably in the spouse's experience.

All of us depend at times on the stability, wisdom, or soothing of our companions, especially when the core of our self is shaken in some way. When my wife gave birth to our handicapped daughter, she was devastated. There was no baby right away to hold in her arms, to cuddle, count toes, and rejoice over. Instead of smiling faces of celebrating visitors, she faced somber eyes of quiet compassion for her and our incubated child. Her fondly rehearsed dreams were shattered. A profound sadness descended upon her, in the midst of which she alternated between feeling let down by God and feeling guilty for having done something wrong. She worried that I would blame her for what had happened and would stop loving her. She worried that she would not have the strength to take our baby home and care for her. At that time, more than at any other time in our marriage, she needed me to comfort and reassure her. In her depleted state, she leaned on me to keep her emotionally together and to take charge of the unexpected turn life had taken. Gradually, as I reassured her of my love and God's, spoke hopefully about our baby's potentials, and provided an atmosphere of order and constancy, she regained her emotional strength, began to dream new dreams, and lovingly cared for our new daughter with unsurpassed tenderness.

The point of this personal story is not that my wife showed weakness at the trauma of our daughter's birth, but that she showed strength. It took strength to reach out, to connect with, and use the support offered by another for her own restoration. That mature capacity is more rare than we think, and is quite different from simply merging into and being pulled along by the willpower of another. As a clergy spouse borrows the strength and hopes of the pastor partner, crises can remain within tolerable limits, becoming passing episodes of life rather than gathered stories of endless woe.

Responses to Disappointment

We all know intellectually that our spouses are human and limited, and yet a part of us is always somewhat shocked when they fail to act as we need or expect. We never get used to the disappointment, even when it becomes predictable. Whether big or small, each injury dampens our spirit a bit and irritates the lining of our sensitivities. We may try to put on a happy face so that our partner will not be driven away by our despondent response, or we may swallow our anger lest we elicit a counterattack that would overwhelm us. But when the core of our self is shaken by the action of one who is part of our core, the principal experiences are forms of despondent withdrawal or rage.

These responses do not have to be overwhelming. If the spouse has the capacity to soothe her or his self, or is able to turn momentarily to others for help in maintaining a balanced perspective, or is graced with firm self-esteem that allows the atoning partner to restore credibility, then the despondency or rage will not obliterate the spouse's understanding spirit. An understanding spirit is a necessary condition for work toward forgiveness and reconciliation. The capacity to re-establish empathic connections once they are broken is the heartbeat of marriage and the only hope for an enduring relationship.

Intense expressions of depressive withdrawal or rage may be normal, however. Take infidelity, for example. A wife typically expects sexual faithfulness from her pastor partner. His marriage vows, signs of loyalty, and pulpit admonitions against adultery create a promise of marital stability. She takes this promise within herself and makes it part of her inner security. In short, the pastor's words and acts of constancy become part of her inner cohesion. His unfaithfulness, therefore, is inevitably a damaging blow to the core of her being. The devastation is often more severe and longer-lasting than would be the case if the pastor died, for besides the shame and self-doubt that arise, all securities become suspect.

This dismembering of one's world can lead to eruptions of rage. The wife of a renowned pastor found out he had been having affairs periodically for many years. In agonizing fury she grabbed his favorite sportcoat, ripped it into pieces, threw it in the toilet, urinated on it, and made her atoning husband pick it out piece by piece. She reported later that this gave her a great deal of satisfaction, and still does when she remembers it. As we have seen, such rage is an attempt not only to strike back at those who have so offended by their unconscionable behavior, but also to shore up and preserve one's rapidly eroding inner core.

This wife's delight in recalling her moment of sweet revenge, however, indicates a common residue: the hurt and rage are never totally drained. There is no such thing as forgiving and forgetting, unless the spouse totally represses the memory or unrealistically disavows its importance. What can be achieved is forgiving and the lessening of pain. That may sound pessimistic, but it is not intended to be. Some clergy couples experience their marriages as stronger and more intimate after going through a crisis like an affair. That is part of God's grace, where suffering deepens understanding and strengthens empathic concern. But in any case, persistent sorrow and rage may surface at times from deep backwood recesses. To use another metaphor, scar tissue forms to close the wound and effect healing, but at times that wound is still sensitive to the touch.

Chronic Idealization Needs

Clergy spouses with chronically weak selves have difficulty living with any tension, lack the ability to soothe themselves, and suffer from inner deadness and meaninglessness. While they may be constantly offering advice to others, they themselves lack the capacity to make decisions confidently. Although they might not recognize it, such individuals rely heavily upon someone else to shore up their frail self-cohesion and to keep their world in order.

That someone else is typically the pastor partner. The spouse may frequently call the church to ask the pastor to come home to deal with: misbehaving children, household chores, repairmen's visits, disturbing calls from a mother-in-law, or an ill pet. If the minister responds that he or she is busy, or that the matter can wait, or that the spouse should take care of it, the spouse reacts with increased anxiety, increased insistence, and perhaps finally with angry outbursts. One wife's archaic expectations were blatantly clear when she said in therapy: "Here I am drinking far more than I should, but he doesn't come home to stop me. He's a minister, for God's sake! He's suppose to know how to save people! He's not the man I thought he was." The reader might suspect, and rightly so, that part of this pastor's avoidance was an expression of passive rage at her. But this does not obscure the point that this wife had mandated him to be her rescuer. Such is the nature of archaic selfobject expectations. Unfortunately, the prognosis for overcoming such disorder of the self is poor, as is the prospect for a happy marriage.

ALTEREGO YEARNINGS

It's normal not to want to share your bed with a stranger. When a clergy spouse rolls over, the face on the next pillow hopefully reflects moods, values, and interests that are comfortingly like the spouse's own. The assurance of that basic similarity allows for tolerance of differences, if not enjoyment of them. On another level, that rudimentary self-sameness wards off the threat of devastating isolation. "I feel like Willy Loman," said one clergy husband, "out on the road, alone, doing my thing all by myself, but not really sharing life with anyone." Being human cannot be borne alone. We need the little noises and sounds of others similar to ourselves.

Moreover, when a spouse takes on new, untried roles or begins some personal exploration—for example, starting work, changing vocations, or beginning psychotherapy—the spouse risks losing a familiar hold on his or her self. Such sojourns into the unknown threaten the ways of feeling and thinking that the self has come to expect. In the excitement of new possibilities, the spouse experiences some apprehension that the self will be lost in the process. While experimenting with new ways of defining the self and new ways of relating to the world, the spouse still has a natural need to preserve the core of his or her present identity and sense of rooted belonging.

A relationship with a sensitive alterego marriage partner helps a clergy spouse maintain self-cohesion. The pastor partner can hold in safekeeping, as it were, those essential characteristics that determine the spouse's identity and belonging, which the spouse is temporarily relinquishing. The spouse has less fear of losing his or her self, trusting that that self can be found again in the alterego partner. "Don't you ever change, even though I do," said one husband with serious humor as he made a midlife career move. "A part of me is afraid that nothing will ever be the same again. Stay as you are, and remind me from time to time who I am when I get anxious." All of us at times are like children who can risk going off to school only as long as they can look over their shoulder and know that they can come back to a mother and a house that will always be the same. The anxiety that one can "never go home again" is often the anxiety that change may come to those people and places one has decreed as permanent repositories of one's identity and belonging.

Disrupted Alterego Relationships

The importance of an alterego partner becomes more obvious when such relationships are altered. For instance, the minister's demanding schedule may leave precious little time for the sharing and playfulness that reinforce the marital friendship. The clergy spouse who feels that the environment threatens his or her personal and social identity may need even more time with the familiar pastor partner, as assurance of belonging and as a sustaining reminder of the normalcy of the spouse's own attitudes and emotional sensitivities.

Loneliness in marriage, however, is not a time problem per se; it is a relationship problem. Often the disturbance has to do with the quality of the couple's alterego bonding. Lack of time together does not necessarily mean the spouse will feel emotionally isolated from the pastor partner, although time apart can make existing loneliness more intense. Obversely, more time spent together does not necessarily lead to marital friendship or growing together. Retirement, for example, does not add anything to a marriage and certainly will not improve a bad one. Many clergy couples, furthermore, have "stuck together" over the years while suffering deep loneliness in the relationship. Loneliness in clergy marriages is related to the quality of the marital bond more than to the quantity of time together. The degree of intimacy is a result of perceived intentions rather than work schedules, conveyed desire rather than disrupted opportunities, the sense of soul-mate connectedness rather than constant physical proximity.

One of the most bewildering disruptions in marriage occurs when the clergy spouse senses that the things the couple had in common have been lost. A worried wife felt increasingly uncomfortable with her pastor partner when they were alone. "We've grown apart to where I don't know what to say to him when we're riding in the car or out to dinner together. He no longer seems interested in the things we both once held so dear, like raising the children, gardening, entertaining friends, and looking forward to vacations alone with each other. Not only am I lonely, but it makes me doubt whether all those things I felt were important really were important. Maybe I was naive. Maybe all that I thought he shared in common with me was just his going along with me, but not really what he wanted." The loss of familiar alterego responses shakes the security not only of the present but of the past and future as well.

A central need of the clergy spouse may be for a partner with similar spiritual and religious convictions. Although it is said that love conquers all, and while couples certainly can accommodate religious differences and still be happy, lack of spiritual unity can be divisive. "I've tried to deny that our religious differences have any bearing on our marital struggles," said one clergy husband. "But they do. My home church and what I was taught are what I'm used to. We fight more about our beliefs and what is right than we find peace in them. I only go to worship services she leads because it would be awkward for her if I didn't. But I feel more like a visitor than a member."

A spouse may also experience loneliness when the minister responds primarily as pastor in the marital relationship rather than as a soul mate. One woman complained, "For some reason he keeps acting like he's still a minister when he's home. I resent it when he takes that pastoral tone with me I've heard him use on others. I'm not just another parishioner he's counseling. I'm his wife, and we're the parents of our children."

When ministers fail to be partners first, their spouses often feel patronized. Ministers minister best at home by being hugging partners rather than acting as family chaplains. Clergy spouses need the *person* of the pastor. A pastor once said, "The tragedy of my life is that although I've led thousands of people to Jesus Christ, I have not been able to save my wife." Perhaps he forgot to be a husband to her first rather than preacher.

Chronic Alterego Needs

Some spouses exhibit chronic needs for near-perfect alterego responses. In therapy, one clergy wife would express a thought and then look at me as if seeking confirmation that I felt the same way. If I did not respond, or if I expressed something different, she would say, "Why can't you see that what I'm saying is true? Why do you always have to interpret it? Whenever you do that I feel you're not with me and that I might as well quit therapy."

That same pressing need for a faithful echo of herself in another made her furious with her husband. "Why can't he run through the fields and flowers with me, freely, spontaneously, like I'd like to? But no. Instead he says, 'Well, just a minute. I'll need to put on my coat and I'll have to make sure I have my boots on.' By that time I'm furious with him and don't want him to come at all." She needed her pragmatic pastor partner to resonate with her own desires to flow freely, to be with her as a companion at play. That need is normal to an extent. But her struggles with disappointing alterego figures early in her life left her defensively insistent on fixed self-same responses and hyper-sensitive to noncompliance.

Her need for him to be her playful alterego encountered his need for her to function in a different selfobject role. Marital disruption occurred not only because of the nature and intensity of her selfobject need, but also because she was linked with a pastor partner driven by his own pressing selfobject requirements. The interfacing of selfobject needs in marriage may take various patterns, as we will see in the next chapter.

SEVEN

Marriage Dances of Clergy Couples

A NY MARRIAGE IS TOO personally meaningful to be reduced to psychological explanations. When you slip your arm around your partner, give a little hug, and whisper tenderly, "I'm lonely for you," your whole body and mind and spirit are in that articulated gesture. You do not reach out to touch a self-object; you do not murmur, "Give me your selfobject presence." You lean with your soul toward this person you love, who is more to you than merely a role or function. If I were to officiate at the reaffirmation of a couple's wedding vows, I would not pronounce a blessing by saying, "And may you express mutual and mature selfobject empathy to each other all your days." Instead I would, with Saint Paul, encourage them with the reminder that love is patient and kind, does not rejoice in the wrong, is not puffed up but endures all things.

This does not mean that analyzing marriage in terms of its psychological processes is worthless or dehumanizing. When you go to a well-known restaurant for delectable cuisine, you immerse yourself in the experience of eating. You give yourself up to the alluring smell of the various dishes, to the sheer pleasure of their taste. This is an occasion of living abundantly. In that occasion, it would be strange for you to say, "They serve good protein here, and the calories are just about right, to say nothing about the acceptable cholesterol level." It would not be wrong to think of the food in terms of its chemical-nutritional value, but it would not be fitting in this circumstance. Too much analysis would cut you off from the simple, lived pleasure of eating. On the other hand—and this is the balancing point—it would not be fitting if we always considered food only in terms of its aesthetic and visceral pleasures. Too much indulgence for enjoyment's sake and we may neglect to analyze our diet in terms of the nutrients necessary for good health.

The same is true with marriage. While there are times when we just need to taste and tussle each other in marriage, at other times we need to stand back and analyze what constitutes that relationship. There should be a fitting rhythm between living marriage and analyzing marriage. Too much examining makes it sterile. Too little examining, however, makes it prey to unseen forces.

Marriage has a sticky coherence. Pastor and spouse are bound together through their normal efforts to maintain the cohesion of their selves, achieved by establishing empathic ties with each other as their supportive selfobjects. In marriage, self-with-selfobject-need meets self-with-selfobject-need. Although it lacks the Bible's poetic imagery, this is the psychological dynamic of husband and wife cleaving to each other.

We will examine clergy marriages as relationships in which pastor and spouse are motivated to find in each other the selfobject support they need for the maintenance of their selves. This approach is not intended to suck the living blood from a personal relationship. The personal meaning of marriage is never exhausted by explanation. Nonetheless, empathic interpretations and explanations can minister to clergy couples who are experiencing marital distress. Clergy couples are strengthened when they feel understood and when their own understanding is broadened.

What organizes and animates a marriage are the patterned ways in which the couple attempts to elicit responses to their selfobject needs. These patterns are like dances. Two people come face to face, expecting the other to be in rhythm with them, expecting to sway harmoniously together. At times the dancers flow gracefully, accommodating each other's movements, in step with the music of each other's needs and hopes. But it is not always so. One partner may eventually become disappointed with the other's two left feet. They may argue about who will lead. One may complain that the partner has but one speed and one dance step for every occasion. They may go through the motions but not really hold each other. They may start to look over the crowd for a new, perhaps secret, dance partner. Strangely enough, if they do not stop dancing and divorce, they will keep going through the familiar steps even if they don't work. Marriage dances established between pastor and spouse are patterned ways the couple goes about attempting to get their selfobject needs met. However graceful or complex the particular dance, this is the basic psychological box step.

The dance patterns we look at here will not be foreign to you. You have observed them in others and have personally experienced them. But now we can understand the deeper meaning of these patterns of striving. Once again we are trying to gain a new perspective by which we can discern the varied expressions of marital life with some depth and clarity.

These marriage dances are not all-inclusive, certainly, and they tend to overlap in the complexity of marital life, but they are major patterns with distinct characteristics. Furthermore, a couple can pass through these patterns or go back to some of them at various developmental stages in their life together. Yet, over time, a couple tends to form a rather stable pattern of relating. Finally, no clergy couple can be summarily categorized via one of these patterns. A couple can, however, broaden their understanding of their life together guided by these descriptions of relating styles.

THE DANCE OF MUTUALITY

A clergy couple may respond to each other's needs with a dance of mutuality. For example, in a marriage where each partner is looking for consistent and adequate affirming responses from the other, a healthy pattern of mutual mirroring may occur. (In the following discussion, *spouse* and *partner* are used as general terms, rather than as referents to noncleric mate and cleric mate.) Although both spouses may have different talents or features they need validated, and while each may look to a different audience, they both thrive on the partner's affirmation of their capacities and achievements. The marriage relationship is sustained as each finds in the other an empathically responding mirroring selfobject.

The clergy couple may be able to form a firmly cohesive mirroring-mirroring marriage. Strokes of praise given by one partner enhance the well-being of the other, who, in the resulting fullness of self, offers returned affirmation. Moreover, each spouse may be able to feel increased pride in the successful accomplishments of the other, just as parents' reservoir of self-esteem rises when their child performs in an outstanding way. Each spouse, therefore, has a stake in the success of the other. As a result, the marriage enjoys a cohesiveness that can endure inevitable injuries from within the relationship and from without.

Each member of the clergy couple may reach out for the comfort and strength of the other. Each spouse more or less expects the other to remain available to help maintain stability when one feels endangered, frustrated, or devitalized. Both pastor and spouse look to be fortified by joining with the power, inspiration, or soothingness of the other.

This couple, therefore, may form a satisfying marriage dance of mutual idealizing. Comforting, reassuring acts from one spouse strengthen the partner, enabling the partner to also be a sustaining presence for the spouse. A pooling of strength stabilizes each and nourishes a partnership that both can count on throughout life. As one pastor said to his wife with a smile, "I guess it's just you and me against the world."

One spouse may look for mirroring responses while the other seeks an idealized figure's responses. A mirroring-oriented pastor can lend strength to the idealizing-oriented spouse, who correspondingly serves to reinforce the pastor's self-esteem. Countless clergy couples have successfully lived out these mirroring-idealizing needs through a dance of mutuality. One contemporary example of this seems to have been the marriage between the late Peter Marshall and his wife, Catherine Marshall. Clearly he fulfilled the role of an idealized source of strength for her, both in life and in death, while she proved to be a figure affirming and even elevating his self in ministry. Pastors and spouses do that for each other every day in countless ways. In this context, of course, a spouse's idealizing need is no more subservient than the partner's mirroring need is dominant. Weakness or strength is not determined by the type of selfobject response a self seeks, but by the maturity of that selfobject need.

This mirroring-idealizing combination has been the classical if not stereotypical relationship of clergy marriages, namely that between a male pastor who expects to be regarded as special·by his wife (and by parishioners), and a wife who expects to experience her husband as an idealized figure whose position and strength contribute to her own sense of well-being. This selfobject-selfobject arrangement has been considered theologically correct by some churches. Through the decades it has been stamped in parishioners' minds as what the norm should be.

Mutuality points to the couple's mature self-self relationship. Here pastor and spouse give each other the necessary support that enables each one's talents and capacities to creatively unfold. For example, in one situation where both husband and wife were ordained ministers, they requested that a congregation not call them as co-pastors. They asked, instead, that the wife be designated the senior pastor, and the husband the associate pastor. The prompting for this came from the husband, who was older and had already served many churches, who now thrilled at the prospect of his newly ordained wife fulfilling her dream of being a senior minister. In this way, her mirroring wishes were directly fulfilled by his support, and his well-being was nourished by joy in her joy.

In mutuality, pastor and spouse are also able to create an atmosphere in which both can believe and accept a number of realities. Neither partner has to insist on his or her own way, but can enter into the lived experience of the other and see through the other's eyes—even while holding on to his or her own perspective. Each affirms the subjective truths and realities of the other. Consequently, a pastor is capable of taking into account the emotional message the spouse is sending, rather than reacting to just the literal message articulated. Instead of instant self-defense, the pastor can look beyond the spouse's railing words to the cry of loneliness or expression of fright in them. In the self-strengthening pattern of mutuality, each partner can tolerate and resonate with the other's view, even when to do so is somewhat painful.

A consistent pattern of mutual responsiveness to each other's self-object needs lays down a deposit of secure feelings that invigorates pastor and spouse and makes it easier to reestablish harmony after the relationship is temporarily disrupted. It was this storehouse of sustaining experiences that Janice and Charles Talbot lacked. As a result, Charles became quickly shaken and enraged when Janice's attentiveness was diverted. Similarly, Janice became quickly shaken and then withdrew when Charles's comforting manner changed. Breaks in the fragile empathic bond led to vilification of the other, rather than to efforts at reconciliation supported by the assurance of each other's love and commitment.

Do marriages marked by the dance of mutuality experience moments of anger or disillusionment? Of course. But the anger is healthy anger. The sharp word or expressed frustration serves a self-righting function; that is, it confronts the partner for the purpose of protecting the integrity of the partner's self, and for preserving the healthy cohesion of the marriage. Disillusionments are absorbed by the empathic partners not as wrenching disappointments but as mature realizations of human finitude.

Clearly this relationship of mutuality has nothing to do with transactions. This is no marital quid pro quo, no attitude of "I'll scratch your back if you'll scratch mine." Instead it has to do with transformations, with attitudes of care for each other that bring about healing and enrichment. It is as if in the spirit of Jesus the spouses live to bring life, and to bring it abundantly.

THE DANCE OF COMPENSATION

Think for a minute about being a parent. The relationship between parent and child is not one of equal mutual influence. A son or daughter as a parent's selfobject does not normally affect the parent's self-esteem or security as much as the parental selfobject affects the budding self of the child. Neither is the manner of being a selfobject for each other the same. The parent does not need the child to wildly applaud a sermon or career accomplishment, but the child may well need the parent's praise for a Little League home run or an A on a report card.

In clergy marriages one partner at times needs to be the stronger one, compensating for the other's temporary loss of self-esteem. This happens normally, for all of us suffer blows to our cherished, often secret self-images. Frequently we then turn to our partner for support. We may even regress a bit, letting out that hurt inner child who simply wants to be taken care of and fussed over. In this state, we may not be able to contribute much to our partner's well-being. Indeed, besides putting our partner's needs on hold, we may actually act in ways that undercut the relationship, even though it has been a good one. We all know, unfortunately, how we say cynical and irresponsible things when we feel our world falling apart. That happens not only because of our diminished ability to control our mood when depressed; it also emerges as an angry protest that looks for someone to make up for the injuries we have had to endure.

If the partner's self is firm enough, then she or he can fill in for the spouse's temporarily impaired capacities for regulating tensions and for self-reassurance. When a proud and vigorous middle-aged pastor found out he needed a heart bypass operation, he became extremely anxious. Not only did old fears about aging and death gnaw away at his confidence, but his self-esteem plummeted by the very fact of finding himself so embarrassingly upset. In this fragmenting state, he worried that the negative voices in the church would take over. He became preoccupied with discussing his condition with parishioners rather than attending to their needs. At times he was short-tempered with his spouse and others. His good wife stood by him lovingly, patiently. She reassured him that he was well loved by the congregation. She reminded him to keep his conversations in appropriate balance, and she tried to be a moderating influence when he became irritated. She functioned to maintain stability in the marriage by continuing normal routines and by taking temporary charge of chores and obligations his depleted self couldn't care less about.

We must note something very important in this touching example. A person can find fulfillment in being an empathic, supportive self-object. The wife here did not feel she was sacrificing herself in giving her jangled husband heavy doses of attentiveness and consolation. Being able to care for him not only felt right, it felt good. The firmness of one's self-esteem, values, goals, and faith can be strengthened by serving as an empathic selfobject for others.

Jesus knew this incomparably. Those who give themselves to others shall find their selves, he taught. His message was never about dissolving or eradicating a person's sense of self. Indeed, it was the preservation and the transformation of the self that he cherished. And one central way in which that happens is by being a sustaining, empathic selfobject. When an individual is too needy, depressed, or angry to give another what the other needs, the power and integrity of both will suffer.

When the self-esteem of the injured spouse has been restored, the clergy couple may well move back to a former pattern of mutuality. That mutuality may take the form of another temporary compensation, where the restored spouse now nourishes the emotionally taxed partner who has kept things together. Once the cohesive balance of both has been reestablished, however, they might resume a quieter, better-functioning pattern of mutually satisfying responses to each other's dominant selfobject needs.

THE DANCE OF COLLUSION

In the collusion dance step, a spouse who feels vulnerable and "weak" depends upon the affirming or guiding acts of the partner, who outwardly appears strong. Lacking self-confidence, the vulnerable spouse endeavors to do whatever is necessary in order to keep the partner acting strong. While enacting the role of the dominant one, the partner in actuality depends upon the subservient praise and dedicated energies from the "weak" spouse. That is, in order to ward off similar internal self-doubts, the partner relies upon the "weak" spouse's continual efforts to make the partner appear, feel, and act strong. Each has a personal stake, therefore, in maintaining this co-dependent, over-adequate-underadequate form of relating. In more or less conscious ways, they collude with each other in order to perpetuate the image of one spouse's neediness and the other's innate strength.

In order to ensure that the partner will continue to function as a mirroring, comforting, or alterego force, the vulnerable-feeling spouse may emotionally cater to the partner. One wife of a clergyman constantly praised her husband, always inquired about his feelings and attitudes, and labored in the home and out to make things comfortable for him. She was an intelligent woman, but as I listened to her talk about her marriage, I pictured an anxious child trying hard to make mother or father feel good so that they could then take care of their child. Indeed, while growing up, the wife had been compelled to bolster her chronically overwhelmed parents. She was their selfobject support rather than they hers. Instead of this experience leaving her with a hard crust of self-reliance, she continued to seek merger with an idealized person who would nurture her. Like other individuals who are frustrated, barren, or insecure, she showed great willingness to promote and follow a supposedly confident partner.

Then again, a spouse may simply remain passive or helpless so that the partner will feel compelled (or enticed) to play the role of the strong one. This becomes most obvious during a crisis. One minister's wife said, "I'm afraid to let him know I'm feeling better inside, because if he thinks I'm strong enough to take care of myself he might leave." At this point, her fear of losing him as her pillar overshadowed the budding awareness that she just might be able to support herself.

If the spouse is severely dependent or has a great fear of being attacked or abandoned by the powerful partner, the subjugation of the spouse's self to the partner's may become pathological. An esteem-impaired spouse may constrict or alter certain needs of his or her self in order not to alienate the partner, or may exaggerate other aspects in order to please and soothe the partner. The spouse may take blame for things that have been caused by the partner, or may defend the partner to others even when the partner has been untrustworthy. Then again, the spouse may turn away from the partner's reprehensible acts toward children and other family members. "Well, I probably did do something to provoke his anger," said one nervous-prone wife. "He's usually right. There probably is something screwed up about how I see things. I guess I haven't been a very good wife."

The overly dependent spouse is not dumb or blind. He or she typically knows that the partner is frequently wrong, too demanding, and unfair. But out of a need to preserve the image of the partner as strong (and thus as a source of strength for the vulnerable-feeling spouse), the spouse acts as if these flaws make no appreciable difference. They are either minimized or are deemed unintended by the partner, and consequently are considered to have no bearing on the marital relationship. The collusion here is a denial that one continues to be self-subjugating, passive, or weak in order to keep the other as a reliably powerful figure one so desperately needs.

The apparently strong partner, however, typically suffers from chronic self-doubts too. Lacking adequate or mature selfobject support from others, the partner turns to the weak spouse, relying upon and fostering the spouse's dependence in order to feel empowered. There is nothing more flattering than to be heralded as a great protector, wise guide, clever wit, or compassionate rescuer. The "strong" partner, therefore, depends upon the dependence of the "weak" one.

The strong partner, however, often disavows this collusion. The partner typically claims that his or her actions are not only benign but loving. "I'm doing it for his own good," said one wife. "If I didn't pick out his clothes and color coordinate them, he'd go to church looking weird. And then where would he be?" By taking care of her spouse rather than helping him learn to care for himself, this wife played into the collusion scheme. She needed to be needed, to the point where she derived more reward in feeling indispensable than in aiding her husband to become self-reliant. That this was a collusive relationship was verified by the absence of protest by the husband. Unlike a growing, self-actualizing youngster who healthily demands, "Let me do it myself," this pastor gave himself up to his wife's motherlike caretaking.

If the "weak" spouse should protest, or begin to grow in emotional ways leading to assertive, even rebellious, attitudes, the "strong" partner typically attempts to preserve the colluding pattern. It is not uncommon for partners to bribe their spouses with promised gifts if they postpone looking for a job, or delay going back to school, or decide against therapy. Even more common is the use of anger and intimidation to keep the spouse in the subjugated position.

The public description that a colluding clergy couple gives of their marriage often does not reveal the true state. Collusive partners often form a kind of united front, proclaiming that everything is fine. They either repress the unhealthy co-dependent acts altogether, or disavow the meaning of these acts, or minimize what meaning they do acknowledge. As a result, well-entrenched collusive couples rarely seek marital therapy. When the co-dependence system starts to break down, however, one partner may bring the other to therapy. Or they may seek help as a couple when apparently tangential problems surface, such as difficulties with a child.

A colluding clergy couple, however, can break out of this pattern. Life's accidents and changes can remobilize energies for self-development, and the presence of new sustaining selfobject persons can open the couple to different styles of dancing.

THE DANCE OF CONTENTION

The partners in a contending clergy couple are engaged in a power struggle with each other. In some way, both spouses try to coerce from the other the recognition, support, or acceptance they feel is their due. The contending may disintegrate into verbal or physical fights, wherein each partner simply attempts to wreak vengeance and injury upon the other. But the contending pattern itself is not simply two persons expressing anger and hostility toward each other. Neither is it always some form of open conflict or confrontation. In contending, each partner attempts to force the needed behavior, attitude, or agreement from the other.

Let's go back to our familiar couple, Janice and Charles Talbot. Throwing the anniversary card at his wife was an expression of Charles's continual anger at her for having ignored him (a mirroring injury). It was also, and principally, a desperate effort to get her to respond to him, to get her to make up to him in a special, conciliatory way other than by giving a demeaning, placating card. Any punishment of Janice or effort to induce guilt in her was not for the ultimate purpose of emotionally destroying her (although she felt destroyed); it was to jar her into compliance, to make her be as he thought she ought to be as his wife.

She contended with him as well, at times verbally accusing him and demanding that things had to change. For the most part, however, withdrawal from him was Janice's instrument of leverage. The withdrawal protected her fragile self from further devastation, while also serving as a passive-aggressive measure intended to force reconsideration on his part. Instead of "throwing at" she was "holding back," denying him her affections and affirmations until he responded as that (idealized) person she needed.

In the contending pattern, active or passive aggression is a signal to the partner for help. The overt form may be demanding or manipulative, yet the covert message is a cry for empathic, in-tune responses. When a pastor or spouse is pumped up with a sense of righteous indignation, however, the act of making an apology, though it may be appropriate, is difficult to do. Making amends leaves one feeling vulnerable to the partner's responses. Fears of future injuries to the self may keep a pastor and spouse from rectifying a situation that could reestablish connectedness. Should this become a chronic situation, the couple may settle into a long-term, low-intensity level of bickering. The couple may seem to get used to this constant feuding, but their children never do. The couple falls into a negative interaction where neither spouse's renewed efforts can penetrate the other's self-protective defense.

Other couples contend without ever raising a voice or fist. Many of you know what it felt like to grow up in a "cold war" home, where mom and dad never fought but where the tension between them was so great that you wished they would yell or throw a plate to relieve the pressure. Just as hard feelings can last a lifetime, so, too, can a pastor and spouse silently contend with each other for year upon year. Even until the last breath, each may wait for the other's confession, apology, or compliance. In this contending pattern, the rise of direct anger may be a potential blessing for the couple, for it may stimulate communication between them, thus offering the possibility of renewed negotiations and satisfactions.

If the contendings are not direct confrontations, or are not reported time and again to others in order to gather sympathetic allies, they are often rehearsed over and over in the partners' minds. Grievances are reviewed, and justifications for one's behavior are reinforced. While these ruminations may have a momentary soothing effect, they eventually spin out into a complex system of thought that may crystallize into such felt truths as, "No one really cares about anybody. Everyone is concerned only with themselves. I'll have to take care of myself and protect myself because no one else cares."

Contending can disintegrate into severe forms of verbal and physical abuse, expressive of the disintegration of the spouses' selves. This is no longer contending; it is combat, the effort to humiliate, discourage, and obliterate the partner. This is rage at its most archaic, regressive level.

THE DANCE OF TRIANGULATION

In the dance of triangulation, the clergy couple attempt to keep their selves cohesive and the marriage intact by incorporating a third entity into their relationship. Marriages, of course, are never just you-and-me affairs. From the first date, relationships with fathers and mothers, brothers and sisters, former girlfriends and boyfriends, shape the young lovers' feelings and fantasies about each other. Marriages stay healthy as pastor and spouse mutually care for a loved one, or share enthusiasm for a valued ideal, or turn to God as the center of their lives. Marriages always include other selves, who are also selfobjects for the couple.

But in the triangulating pattern described here, the couple draw a third into their interpersonal world, not as a healthy extension of the couple's mature bonding, but as the glue they hope will fuse their weak union or keep their vulnerable individual selves from fragmenting. Couples tend to incorporate a third when they fear their marriage is dangerously close to dissolving. How common it is to hear, "Maybe if we had a baby it would draw us closer together." Another couple may say, "Maybe if we moved to a new church, things would be different between us." Here the baby or new church is expected to bring cohesion to a feeble or unfulfilled marriage, rather than being a joyful expression of united hearts.

Activities can also function in the same way. The marriage becomes focused around the activity—going to flea markets, or working on antique furniture, or exercising—rather than the activity being an extension of a solid emotional bond between pastor and spouse. If the activity ends or becomes boring, the relationship's vitality dwindles proportionally. Too often the activity of church work becomes the cement intended to hold a clergy couple together, giving them a semblance of togetherness when in fact they have no real core of abiding connectedness. "We have our work" may express a rich companionship based on a shared commitment, or it may represent two people who have no emotional substance between them except a common project.

Then again, triangulating can be an avoidance of dangerous involvements by putting something between the couple. Focusing on a disruptive child, for instance, can deflect the partners' explosive anger at each other onto the third. Conversely, focusing excessive love and affection on a child may be a way of avoiding marital intimacy, especially if such intimacy threatens the security of the pastor or spouse. Fears of hostility as well as fears of closeness can lead couples to triangulate other distractors into their shaky interpersonal world.

Couples may triangulate others for the avowed purpose of enhancing the relationship. The partners may expect an infusion from outside to bring renewal to their stagnating relationship. When the marriage is failing to generate the emotional energy the spouses need from each other in order to ward off anxious self-doubts, they may engage a third in order to "heat up" the relationship. Relating with "swinging" couples, or out-and-out spouse-swapping, may be desperate efforts to funnel excitement into the marriage. The new ways of seeing one's spouse in action may also recast the partner into an attractive object of desire. If the cohesion of the couple's selves are chronically vulnerable, they may engage in a wide variety of triangulations in an effort to ignite a marital fire.

Finally, couples employ the triangulating pattern when the stress of serving as a sustaining selfobject feels too demanding. There's an old story about a man who took his depressed wife to a therapist. After talking to them together, the perceptive therapist asked the wife to stand up. He took her in his arms and gave her a warm, reassuring hug. For the first time in months a smile appeared on her face, and worry wrinkles around her eyes began to disappear. The therapist turned to the husband and said, "Now you can clearly see what your wife needs." The husband replied, "Well, OK. But I can only bring her in on Tuesdays and Thursdays."

Unfortunately, the expectation that others will stand in as substitute selfobjects is not rare. When our drives for mirroring, idealizing, or alterego responses outside of marriage make us impatient with the needs of our spouse, or when we feel unable to provide the kind of support our spouse requires, then alternative thirds are sought in order to reduce marital tensions and responsibilities. For example, a mirror-motivated, workaholic pastor, preoccupied with his "mistress" the church, encouraged his nurturant-seeking wife to form other friendships in order for her to receive the tender regard she needed, which he was tired of supplying. Feeling that she was "too needy," and that her needs were "taking him away from the work he was called to do," she did begin to search for other individuals who could provide daily doses of reassuring human contact. It is true that clergy couples cannot realistically expect to have all emotional needs met by their partners. But in triangulating marriages, this truism becomes a justification for turning to outsiders as one spouse relinquishes selfobject responsibility for the other.

A sexual affair may not be a form of triangulation, even though both partners will be affected by the act. When one mirror-seeking minister was promoted to a position of great prominence, his grandiose self became so expansive, so filled with sensations of power and special-ness, that he gave himself up to the allurement of a woman who expressed desire for him. While his marriage was under some pre-existing tension, it became clear during his work in therapy that the affair emanated from his momentarily excessive grandiose feelings.

When an affair is an expression of rage at the spouse, as well as an effort to wrench new behaviors and attitudes from the violated spouse, this is part of a contending pattern. When one spouse, however, turns away from blatant signs of the other's affair, this may express an existing collusion pattern. When the couple has so detached themselves from each other that they consider sexual-romantic involvements with oth-ers as "getting on with our lives," this is perhaps more an expression of a divesting pattern.

THE DANCE OF DIVESTMENT

Divesting is not simply withdrawing. A pastor can still have great investment in his or her spouse but withdraw in hurt or self-pity, or withdraw as a way of trying to get the partner to come around (a form of contending). In the divesting pattern, energy is extracted, as it were; hope, meaning, significance, allurement, sometimes even bitterness felt for the partner is removed from that person as a selfobject. In certain relationships divesting is a healthy, self-preserving action. For example, a spouse who finally detaches emotionally from a partner who has been chronically abusive is pulling away from an archaic and debilitating relationship. But the divesting pattern here described is one in which the vitality felt for and given to the other is drained off, with only the shell of the partner or the marriage expected to remain intact.

We have all seen these marriages. A pastor says of his wife, "She's a good mother, good housekeeper, and good church member, but I no longer have any personal feelings for her. I no longer turn to her for any of my emotional needs." "Something has died between us," responds the wife, "although we still go through the motions. We live like brother and sister, or even worse, like tenants who simply share the same house, living our own separate lives. We expect little from each other except not to make waves."

Clergy couples who are no longer drawn together by selfobject longings often remain married. The marriage structure then serves purposes other than the reciprocal fulfillment of self-needs. Clergy couples stay married "because of the children," or because if they got a divorce "the church would ask us to leave, and it would be difficult to find another position, which we simply couldn't afford." Marriages of necessity, or marriages for convenience, or marriages out of duty characterize many clergy couples.

While each spouse may divest energy from the whole person of the partner, some divest energy only from part of the person. Our selfobject grasp of the other—the way we reach out to make that person an extension of us—may include the whole of that person or only part. In difficult times, couples may normally divest importance in each other as whole persons to focus on the functions or roles each can provide. The relationship shrinks, to the point where each partner feels little empathy for the other's dreams or current sadnesses, but expresses concern only for the other's fulfillment of responsibilities at home or at work. When self-cohesion returns, however, the partner as a total person may be reinvested with deeper meaning and importance. The parameter of the relationship expands once again to include the whole range of the partner's being and becoming.

Permanent divestment from whole to part also occurs, however. One clergy wife realized that over the years she had come to relate to her husband as a function rather than as a person. She needed him to provide the soothing and comfort that she missed from her obsessively preoccupied mother, but she was not attached to him personally. She kept investment in only part of him, namely in his role of providing reassurance. She had no tolerance, therefore, for his style of life, nor real interest in a sexual life with him, but was concerned only with that part of him that could help her, as she put it, "keep the bunkers of my life from crashing in." An extensive part of her nuclear self was isolated from a full, interpersonal relationship.

A divesting pattern may be an original dance rather than a developed one. If the selves of the clergy couple have been severely disordered since childhood, they may lack the ability to form a mature relationship. A weak capacity to seek mirroring responses may come from traumatic injuries to self-esteem during childhood. Mistrust and low-intensity idealizing may prevail due to absent or abusive parental figures. Avoidance of alterego alliances may reflect an early hopelessness of ever feeling accepted.

VARYING AND MIXING
THE STEPS

Dance steps vary within each pattern, of course. In the collusion pattern, for instance, a couple may periodically alternate between playing the weak and the strong roles. We have noted some of the variations possible in the contending pattern. The general principles, nonetheless, still abide.

Patterns are often mixed in a marriage as well. One partner may be contending while the other is divesting—a common mixed pattern. One spouse may be fostering mutuality while the other operates from patterned actions expecting compensation.

The point throughout, however, is that a clergy couple engages each other in patterned ways, by which they hope to find in each other adequate responses to their selfobject needs. An understanding of these dynamics will hopefully assist the couple in broadening their empathy for each one's own self and for the self of the other.

PART THREE
Viewing Parishes

E I G H T
The Crowd Around Jesus

I N MATTHEW 15:29-30 we read these words: "[And Jesus] went up the mountain, where he sat down. Great crowds came to him." Note that last phrase: "Great crowds came to him." In the deepest religious sense that is what the church is, a gathered crowd around Jesus, like those the Gospel describes as sitting at Jesus' feet. Here to the mountain of the church building people come regularly, rubbing shoulders, huddling down, ready to learn from Jesus and be led by him. However well orchestrated our worship may be, however dignified we might act, we are nothing more sophisticated than a crowd hungering for divine words of life. Our effort in these next two chapters is to understand the inner workings of this crowd gathered around Jesus.

THE CONGREGATION AS A
GROUP SELF

Do you remember a little sing-song hand game you probably played as a child: "Here is the church" (fingers interweave), "and here is the steeple" (index fingers rise and meet), "open the door" (palms turn upward), "and see all the people" (fingers wag in greeting). What kind of impression did you have about "all the people"? I remember imagining my fingers as individuals, some as dads and moms, others as kids, some as old people, a few as visitors. But at the same time, it seemed to me that all those member fingers were the same, or at least much alike, and that they formed a unit, an indivisible whole, as concrete and permanent as the church building and its steeple.

Both of these perceptions about a church are accurate. On the one hand, a parish is a collection of whole beings, a gathered pluralistic community where individuals, each with a personal identity and private needs, come together. In this light it is appropriate to focus on parishioners as individual selves, who, just like the pastor and spouse, struggle to maintain self-cohesion by finding supportive selfobject figures. While other persons in the parish can serve as needed selfobjects for an individual parishioner, most commonly the parishioner turns to the pastor (and often the pastor's spouse) as the special figure from whom mirroring, idealizing, or alterego responses are expected. When a clergy couple enter a parish, they are inevitably cast, to some degree, into this role of fulfilling the parishioner's selfobject needs. Clergy marriages come under stress when individual parishioners press pastor and spouse for performance of these selfobject roles, and when they react with varying degrees of rage or depressive withdrawal when the clergy couple fail in their task.

But the church is also a whole collection, a functioning psychological unit with a life of its own that includes but transcends the individuals comprising it. In the language we have been using, the church is also a self, a group self. Consider this situation.

The president of Westwood Community Church sought emergency counseling. "We're falling apart," he exclaimed. "A large majority of the people call Reverend Estevez a devil who is destroying our church. A vocal minority support him and his work. Each group is at the other's throat. The life of the church has dwindled down to nothing more than preoccupation with this issue. We've got to do something!"

Later accounts from the gathered church council revealed that Westwood had been an old rural congregation made up basically of members raised in the church, many whose mothers and fathers had literally built the church plank by plank. Parishioners had a deep affinity for the building, parish life, and for one another. Worship, programs, and social activities were shaped around the familiar rhythms and themes of rural life. The parish expected their pastor to be "like them," to the point where he was directed to wear jeans and flannel shirts as his daily garb, rather than a business suit.

Rapid industrial development in the area resulted in unexpected church growth for Westwood. Within a few years, new individuals had joined the church and become vocal members. These persons brought not only increased dollars into the church but also new ideas, expectations, and demands. The comfortable, familiar atmosphere began to change, as did the range and type of programs offered.

As I listened to the story of Westwood as a rural congregation, I sensed that this parish had not been a collection of diversified individuals. There had been a cohesion to this multiplicity of persons, a feeling of continuity through time, and a particular way in which they seemed bonded together. At the present moment this bond was being threatened with disintegration. The most empathic way I could understand and explain the nature of that group wholeness was by visualizing the parish as a self. Conceptually stated, the psychological structure and form of Westwood as an institutional gathering of parishioners over time was its group self.

To say that a church is a self erroneously suggests an equation between the terms *church* and *self.* The self does not worship; it does not proclaim the Word, celebrate the sacraments, and equip believers for ministry and witness. The church as a faithful crowd around Jesus acts in this personal way. Instead, it is more accurate to say that a church functions as a self. The church's self is its organized and organizing psychological core. The self of the church is that church's personality, its unique makeup over time, its cohesive way of responding and acting in the world. As a bishop once said to me, "I can follow the history of a church for twenty, thirty, even a hundred and fifty years and it seems to have the same corporate personality."

SELFOBJECT NEEDS OF THE CONGREGATION

Why is the concept of the congregation as group self relevant for clergy marriages? Because clergy marriage in the context of parish life is complicated, and because pastor and spouse need all the explanatory help they can get in order to stay healthy. Pastor and spouse meet not simply individual needs of particular parishioners, but particular selfobject expectations from the congregation as a whole. A church has a self, analogous to the pastor's and spouse's selves. The church's primary psychological aim is to maintain self-cohesion by connecting with empathically responding selfobject figures. Pastors and spouses become the primary figures who are to provide normal mirroring, idealizing, or alterego responses. At other times they are expected to compensate for disappointing pastors and spouses in the congregation's past. They may be expected to fulfill excessive demands when the parish is falling apart. When pastor and spouse fail in their expected role, the parish responds with a wide range of rageful or withdrawing acts. Pastors are seldom aware of these lurking dynamics when they enter a parish. Informed anticipation can mitigate potential injuries.

In various situations a congregation will expect the pastor (or spouse) to enhance the parish's reputation, or to be available for comforting solace, or to empty himself or herself and become one with the parishioners. Close observation of congregational life, however, generally indicates that the self of a parish tends to revolve around a particular selfobject need.[14] A parish tends to have a dominant self-object need that animates its life, and to which it is most sensitive.

For instance, Westwood as a rural parish self seemed to have been formed primarily around the need to express and enhance its alterego bonding. Mirroring needs did not appear prominent, nor were longings for an idealized pastor or clergy couple dominant. In the past, Westwood had been served by ministers reflecting the essential sameness of its members. As alterego selfobjects, the pastors had preserved and enhanced the alterego style of the parish.

Reverend Estevez, however, came to Westwood with strong needs to be in charge and do things his way, reflecting his core need for mirroring. The influx of new people who did not share the parish's history and alterego alliances, combined with the ascendancy of a selfobject-alien pastor, threatened Westwood's once well-formed core. Rage in the form of excessive accusations and retaliation arose as the old church contingent fought to reinstate the primacy of its alterego aims and programs.

SELF-COHESION OF PARISHES

As is the case with individuals, a central feature of the parish is the quality of its self-cohesion. Some churches enjoy firm, reliable self-cohesion. They tend to be resilient in the face of threats to their self-image, their ideals and hopes, and their sense of being acceptable. When injured in some way, they do not become decimated but continue to function adequately and minister sensitively. These churches are able to form basically mature relationships with their pastors and the pastors' spouses, wherein they respond with empathy and measured frustration when these individuals act in disappointing ways.

At the other extreme, some parishes exhibit chronically weak or inadequately structured selves. They typically have histories of unsuccessful relationships with pastors, tend to respond to difficult situations with despondency or outrage, seem unable to utilize the guidance of helping others, and create a general atmosphere of aimlessness, rigidity, or anger.

Parishes vary in the nature of their group cohesiveness. All religious communities, however, experience fluctuations in their self-cohesion from time to time, as every congregation, clergy member, and clergy spouse knows. Just like individuals, parishes are inevitably vulnerable to selfobject injuries, and are thus given to some expression of rage or depressive withdrawal.

It seemed clear, for example, that the group self of Westwood was in a state of disintegration. The parish's capacity for self-soothing was diminished, as evident in parishioners' wide-ranging efforts to hurt anything attached to the pastor. Its ability to observe and to employ reality-testing was diminished, as shown in the rise of disturbed and regressive thought processes (such as in its paranoid-like statements that the pastor was a devil, and in its boundless blaming and obsessive preoccupations). Neither could it maintain a sense of bodily wholeness (schism in the church), nor act with sustained empathy (calling disagreeing others the enemy).

How the parish structures its relationship with the pastor and pastor's spouse can be understood as a reflection of the state of its self. That is, the type of relationship a church creates with its pastor is based upon: (1) the parish's central selfobject expectations toward the pastor (and spouse), and (2) the quality of the parish's self-cohesion, which shapes how those expectations are expressed. The next chapter briefly describes the range of mirroring, idealizing, and alterego expectations the parish self has for pastor and spouse. Understanding these expectations will prepare us to look at the active, triangular life among pastor, spouse, and congregation.

N I N E
Faces of the Bride

PARISHES NEED CLERGY. They need someone who will make them feel special. They need someone they can look up to. They need someone who is like them. The dossiers of some churches seem to have "admire us" written across their pages, with the expectation that the pastor (and spouse) will serve in a manner that will represent, maintain, and enhance the parish's self-esteem. The dossiers of other churches have "love us" penned between the lines, with the expectation that the pastor (and spouse) will reach out in soothing, strengthening, uplifting ways. The dossiers of other churches have "join us" embossed on their sheaves, with the expectation that the pastor (and spouse) will foster feelings of identity, belonging, and normalcy in the parish by becoming a kindred parish soul.

The needs of a parish for mirroring selfobjects, idealized selfobjects, and alterego selfobjects are normal. No parish is without its own selfobject expectations, any more than an individual is without self-object yearnings. These are the basic psychological attachments in life. The crucial issue is how intense these expectations and yearnings are. The more fragile a parish's self is, the more reliant that parish is upon its selfobject figures for preserving the parish's self-cohesion and self-esteem. The church as the bride of Christ has many faces.

MIRRORING EXPECTATIONS

In understanding the relationship between a local parish and its clergy couple, it is less helpful to think of the pastor and spouse as discrete objects separate from the parish, than to consider the pastor and spouse as extensions of the parish, as the parish's selfobjects. In what follows we see how the parish implicitly makes the pastor and the spouse its selfobjects, extensions of its world, who are supposed to respond fittingly to the parish's mirroring, idealizing, or alterego needs.

Pastor as Mirroring Selfobject

All churches expect their pastor to act in ways that will make them feel proud. Implicitly they anticipate that the minister will project an image of friendliness and competency in the public domain, which will enhance the parish's self-esteem. It is normal for parishioners' hearts to swell with delight when the pastor's reputation for leading worship or conducting weddings and funerals is widely admired.

A parish's primary selfobject expectation may be for its pastor to respond to its core need for affirmation. When a church's self-cohesion has been firmly established, the tie to an affirming pastor is required principally for maintaining the positive feelings the church generally has about its self. That is, the actions and words of the pastor are not necessary for keeping the church glued together, but they support the church's own healthy self-esteem. An analogy would be a spouse who is productively engaged in life activities and only needs the partner's confirming response to augment his or her own internal sense of satisfaction.

A mirror-oriented parish will be particularly drawn to pastors who seem capable of contributing to the parish's feeling of specialness. Negatively stated, the parish will be vigilant for pastors who may prove an embarrassment to it. In interviewing a pastoral candidate, for example, the search committee not only listens for an outstanding voice and sermon delivery, but also scrutinizes the pastor's physical appearance, style of dress, and subtle mannerisms.

Mirror-sensitive churches are reluctant to hire ministers with handicaps, or male pastors with feminine traits, or homosexual clergy, or (in some cases) female pastors. While there may be idealizing and alterego reasons for these negative preferences, they often stem from the anticipation that such pastors will not only fail to enhance or restore a parish's self-image, but will actually be a detriment to it. In the same way that a hypersensitive spouse experiences the partner's acts not just as the partner's own doing but as aspersions on the spouse's personal self, so, too, are the characteristics of the pastor considered potential blotches on the parish's reputation. When the pastor does fail in the role of a mirroring selfobject, the parish responds with varying degrees of rage or despondency—as all individuals and groups do to felt injury.

Some churches are chronically vulnerable and demand that the pastor be but a mirroring extension of itself. Leaders of one church said with confrontational boldness, "You are to be here for us, not us for you." Or again as the consistory of another church intoned, "Remember, you are just a hired hand here." In these cases the selfobject role of the pastor is reduced to nothing more than a job function. It is as though the parish no longer deems the personal side of the pastor as part of the qualities they rely upon, but instead focuses solely on the pastor's mandated duties as the measure of his or her importance. The impact of this attitude upon the pastor's self-esteem, and upon the cohesion of the pastor's marriage, is formidable.

Hopefully a parish self will enjoy a healthy sense of grandiosity. In the movie *Chariots of Fire,* the athletic preacher says with dignified humility, "When I run, and run fast, I feel God's pleasure." With the same mature grandiosity, a parish may feel God's pleasure when they "run the race" with great public and denominational success.

A parish's insufficiently regulated grandiosity, however, may result in debilitating actions. Acting as if it were smarter than other parishes or a step ahead of its denominational leaders, the church may fail in reality-testing—for example, working on its own biased and inaccurate assumptions as to what is best, right, and necessary for others. A parish self groupthink may arise, a rigid perspective that shuts off dissent and thus, in the absence of contradictory data, concludes that its perspective is validated. The parish then expects the pastor to be an implementer of its plans and policies, and becomes irritated when the pastor attempts to insert a new or contrary viewpoint.

Spouse as Mirroring Selfobject

Most churches no longer assume that the pastor's spouse (historically a wife) will be an unpaid assistant in the church, leading Sunday school, playing the organ, and organizing church suppers. But as a minimum, parishes certainly expect the spouse to affirm the importance of the pastor's work and to convey an appreciation for the life of the church. Such confirmations of the church's worth may come through the spouse's attendance at services, by a friendly attitude toward parishioners, and by some participation in church activities. In this sense, all parishes anticipate being mirrored by the generally supportive demeanor of the pastor's spouse.

These low-energy mirroring acts are sufficient for some churches with firm self-cohesion. Their mirroring needs tend to be mild to modest. They enjoy reliable self-esteem built from adequate mirroring responses from past selfobject figures. When, for example, the spouse does not attend church regularly, or participates minimally, the church feels hurt but is not unduly disturbed. The congregation may exhibit tolerance for the spouse's decision, along with a separate regard for the pastor as an individual and professional.

But a mirror-sensitive parish may be much more unsettled by such acts by the clergy spouse. Church attendance may be the very least that is required. Spouse and children may also be called upon to set good examples. How the children misbehave in church and out, how the spouse dresses, what type of work the spouse pursues as a means of income, or how the spouse answers the phone curtly—all these may be experienced as thorns in the flesh of a mirror-sensitive congregation. Gossip may abound. Such behavior can become the topic of conversation in pastoral relations committees. Pastors may even be directed to straighten out the family or else find another church.

A parish may be tolerant of the spouse's minimal involvement in the parish, on the one hand, or may be very exacting, on the other, or may be somewhere in between. But parishes seem inclined to find someone who will serve in the role of pastor's spouse. Protestant parishes have become accustomed to having a minister's wife in the parsonage home, who provides a symbolic, if not pragmatic, feminine presence for the congregation. The pastor's wife embodies the feminine side of feelings, to which parishioners can relate. She may be counted on to provide feminine touches to parish meetings and social gatherings.

In a sense, there is no parish without a female spouse or substitute. In churches where the pastor is single, someone fills the selfobject role of the feminine presence, whether it be a church secretary, deaconess, nun, or other strong laywoman. In Protestantism, an ordained female associate often fills that function, especially if the male pastor is single or his wife is minimally involved in church life. A case might also be made for the parish self needing the presence of a selfobject masculine presence. The point is that spouses are not dispensable in the parish. Their unique personalities, concrete involvements, or symbolic presences become the selfobject material the parish uses to preserve its self-cohesion and self-esteem. Inadequate mirroring responses lead to tensions in the parish-spouse relationship, consequently affecting the pastor and spouse.

IDEALIZING HOPES

Like an individual, a parish longs to be attached to powerful, uplifting figures. A congregation normally looks to the pastor to spiritually inspire them, to create an atmosphere in worship where persons feel God's closeness and care. When tragedy strikes and the grief of church members is too deep to be articulated, the parish turns to the pastor for a warm word that names their pain and holds out hope. When changes disrupt the expected routine of parish life, the parish leans on the confident, steady hand of the pastor to see it through. For many churches the pastor is that figure of respect whose capacities to inspire, to stand firm in the face of stress, and to embody values of the highest order are embraced by the parish self, becoming the foundation of its sense of vitality, tranquility, and commitment in the world.

Pastor as Idealized Selfobject

The parish's primary selfobject expectation for the pastor may be that he or she fulfill the role of this idealized sustaining figure. A parish enjoying firm self-cohesion may only need the presence of an idealizing pastor in order to maintain an inner sense of calm and conviction. That is, rather than relying totally on the minister to reassure and consolidate the parish, the parish is capable of self-soothing and self-direction, fortified by the comforting presence of the revered pastor.

An idealizing-oriented parish, however, may look to borrow guiding values and hopes from the pastor. Lacking the capacity to give themselves direction or to be uplifted by their own espoused beliefs, they attempt to overcome the mounting internal distress by embracing the confident, faith-filled spirit of the minister. In such a state, a parish hungers for reassuring words, as are found in portions of this pastoral prayer for a struggling congregation.

> Dear God, who has seen us safely through the night, and who has been lovingly present with those whose night was their last, we can but put ourselves in your care and protection. We cannot help but be afraid about getting sick, about unexpected things upsetting our life traumatically. But without the assurance that you are always with us, our common anxiety becomes great seizures of distress. Stay close to us that

we might stay calm. When we feel so good and so powerful that we forget about you and think we need no one else, humor us, be patient with us, as a good parent is with a headstrong child. Thank you for those days and weeks where life stays routine, where we are able to be flexible and adaptive to changes, where concerns about health and finances are minimal if not absent. Thank you for laughter and light moments, for beauty that literally makes us gasp, and for the friendly, embracing arms of this church.

If the loss of self-cohesion is only temporary, such as normally happens during times of transition in the life of a church, the pastor's adequately nurturing responses may stabilize the parish self, allowing it to regain its momentum and self-assurance. The pastor functions, then, as a holding environment, whose nonanxious presence soothes souls and summons resurrected hopes. This often is the role of interim clergy, who come to hold hands and hold things together until the parish feels able to walk on its own again.

The more a parish self lacks inner balancing capacities and strong guiding ideals necessary for firm self-cohesion, however, the more intensely expectant that parish may be. Parishes, for instance, may expect the pastor to be its agent of confrontation: to deal forcefully with an errant choir director or funeral director; to fight with school officials when they set up programs interfering with established church activities; to stand up for the underdog; or to challenge the denomination's policies. Parishes rally around a figure whose strength promises to give them strength.

Fragmentation-prone parishes may give themselves up to the leadership of powerfully acting pastors, whose unflagging physical energy and utter self-confidence stir the blood of the anemic congregation. In some severe cases like this, devastation may result, such as in the submission of the people to the demonically charismatic "Reverend" Jim Jones in Guyana in 1978. In many cases, however, the spiritual transfusion simply fails. The pastor's initially good presentation is often a cover for inner uncertainty, and eventually the grasping hand of the parish reaching out for support meets the empty hand of the pastor stretching back. Chronic disillusionment may lead the parish to hire and fire a series of senior and associate ministers in a frenetic search for one who will empower them permanently. In this volatile situation, a pastor is ascribed with sainthood one week and satanhood the next.

Spouse as Idealized Selfobject

A "P.K." church secretary in her early sixties tells how her mother was always referred to as Mrs. Kranz. "That title of respect was granted her because she was the pastor's wife. And it extended over to us kids. We, too, were treated well and shown some deference because we were the 'preacher's kids.' "

Is the minister's spouse still put on a pedestal because of her attachment to the pastor? (We will speak primarily of wives here because the data on clergy husbands are still out.) Is she still initially idealized for no other reason than what we might call her affinity with reverence? To some degree, yes. Parishes still tend to baptize each new pastor with sprinkles of specialness that drip even upon the spouse's head. Initially, a general attitude of respect is given to the clergy spouse.

Parishes are sophisticated about the pastor's spouse. They acknowledge that the spouse might be employed outside the home. They know the spouse may allot limited time to church activities. They accept that it is healthy for the spouse to be her or his own person, rather than a mere extension of the pastor. But a "holy helpmate" image still lodges in the psyche of Protestant churches. Parishes harbor vague to clearly articulated desires for the pastor's spouse to be loving and giving, to be actively involved in church work rather than secular work, to make the parsonage a hospitable home where all are welcome, and to be an inspiring figure others can learn from. The memories of cherished clergy spouses in the past may rekindle anticipations of the same when a new pastor arrives. On the other hand, past failures of clergy wives may mobilize restitution fantasies in the parish; that is, expectations that this spouse will make up for disappointments suffered from predecessors.

Idealization-leaning parishes with firm self-cohesion may primarily expect the spouse to fulfill her selfobject role in specific situations, rather than being ubiquitously available. For instance, while the spouse may work outside the home, the parish may need to see the wife at least graciously accompany the pastor to special church gatherings in order for the parish to maintain internal feelings of completeness and harmony. The image of a united couple is a powerful symbol for persons and communities. Probably representing the security and nurturance of yoked parents, the presence of a united (and idealized) couple tends to stir early experiences of being cared for and nurtured. The togetherness of the pastoral couple kindles hopes in the parish that it, too, will enjoy togetherness. The presence of the spouse, therefore, even on a limited basis, is not without significant selfobject meaning.

Idealization-hungry parishes, with less firm self-cohesion, may yearn for more consistent participation from the spouse. They may hope she will accompany her husband on home visitations, or will be present between services to confide in, or be available to call on in the event of crises. In this idealizing state, the parish may acknowledge that a spouse has personal needs, but may mistakenly assume that the spouse already has as much religious and social support as she needs.

Idealization-demanding parishes may show little tolerance for deviance from the expected role. Little leeway may be allowed for acts of indiscretion or for emotional difficulties. Parishes may expect the spouse to be religiously and socially self-sufficient. As the parish feels stretched beyond its limits, as its own functioning and capacity for self-soothing are depleted, greater and greater pressure may be placed on the spouse to respond with reassuring acts of competency and compassion.

ALTEREGO YEARNINGS

When I prepare to step into the pulpit of my church, I automatically operate from an awareness of how it experiences itself as a community. In the background of my mind, I am aware of the church's German heritage, of its evangelical but liberal theological persuasion, of its association with a college—all of which are part of its present identity. As I prepare the sermon, I am implicitly attuned to its general social and intellectual orientation, knowing what will be too preachy, too childish, too political, or too abstract. When I write up the order of service, I am cognizant of those traditions, familiar rituals, beloved hymns, and patterns of worship that have been part of its communal experience for many years.

Every parish has its own history, traditions, practices, skills and talents, religious orientation, theological perspective, intellectual level, economic status, and racial-ethnic cast, which are experienced as intrinsic to its very being. The enactment and the maintenance of this communal culture links the community together, giving it a more or less firm sense of being one, of being fused together by an essential sameness. The alterego bonding of the parish creates experiences of a shared identity, of a shared sense of belonging, and of a shared assurance of wholesomeness.

Pastor as Alterego Selfobject

A parish self remains firm when selfobject figures respond empathically to its alterego life by joining with its cherished symbols and practices and by fortifying alterego bonds when necessary. The pastor is that central figure to which the parish looks for needed alterego responses. As the pastor is able to empathically join with the parish's alterego self, the parish's experiences of shared identity, belonging, and wholeness are preserved.

Some parishes with firm self-cohesion require only limited alterego responses from the pastor to maintain the vibrancy of their alterego bonds. The pastor's self-sameness with them complements their experience of communal solidarity rather than constitutes it. A healthily integrated church was pleasantly surprised when a new, unknown interim pastor recounted in his opening sermon how a founding family of that church were the ancestors of a child who three generations later went into the ministry and who, by providence, now stood before them as their preacher. That link with the history of the church not only went a long way toward making him an acceptable part of the parish, but it also tickled the alterego bones of the church, making it smile with satisfaction. His affinity with the church, however, was not required in order for the church to feel confident that it would not lose its identity.

All parishes undergo some threat to their alterego core from time to time and thus experience various degrees of fragmentation. The racial makeup of a congregation may change, threatening its homogeneous identity. Its theological orientation may become critically devalued in the ebb and flow of public and ecclesiastical opinion. A new choir director or organist may discard church music that parishioners consider sacred. Whenever transitions occur in a parish, the old ways are in danger of being diminished if not dying.

Here the parish turns to the pastor to be an alterego curator. Acting as the parish's alterego, the pastor represents and thus reinforces its identity, strengthens its sense of group loyalty, and gives assurances that its particular self-same needs are normal. Perhaps the most common mistake pastors make coming into new parish situations is the failure to initially function as an empathic alterego, the failure to join in and celebrate the parish's established ways of life.

Increased threats to a parish's alterego bonds result in increased dependence upon the pastor to function as a sustaining alterego. The minister will be called upon to preserve if not reconstruct those practices that have given assured identity, belonging, and wellness to the congregation. For instance, St. John's began as a fledgling congregation whose cohesiveness was formed around alterego connections. Young families, looking for companionship and support in a town known for its lack of community, rallied around plans to build a church. The building project provided the occasion for establishment of belonging, identity-giving relationships. Members pledged together their monies, immersed themselves in one another socially, and labored side by side on the new church. Throughout this early stage in the parish life, forms of worship, calendars of social activities, decision-making processes, and expectations of how the pastor was to conduct the ministry were motivated by this underlying need for alterego bonding. The persistent image used to describe their group self was "We are a family."

Later, as the church building was completed, the excitement wore off. The pastor left. The financial grind of meeting mortgage payments set in, and the alterego solidarity of the church began to crumble. Fun events became of necessity fund events. Unrest caused some members to leave, disrupting the sense of fused loyalty, making a balanced budget more difficult to achieve, and perpetuating a spiral of demoralization. Members who recalled those early blissful days yearned for a return to them. When a new pastor was called, St. John's laid upon him the task of reestablishing the family atmosphere. He was not only to join what remnant of alterego bonding remained, he was to restore the original climate of communal identity, belonging, and wholesomeness. Understandably, despair and anger arose when his agenda for the church did not match theirs.

In a desperate effort to maintain its core, a parish self may move to an isolationist position in order to protect its identity. Here the pastor may be expected to function as a near-perfect echo of the parish. The pastor may be directed to dress the same as parishioners, to live in a house no better and no worse than homes of parishioners in general, to reside in the same neighborhood as the parish, and so on. Parishes that exhibit weak or diffuse alterego alliances are often parishes that have suffered irreparable damage to their sense of community.

Spouse as Alterego Selfobject

The need to have one's humanness with others quietly acknowledged is a basic need. Situations arise in the everyday life of the parish where parishioners are strengthened not through mirroring that attests to their competence and achievement, not through the calming effect that comes from joining an idealized figure's greater power, but through their being quietly sustained by someone in whose presence they feel at one. That feeling of acceptance, belonging, and normalcy comes about as the alterego selfobject fits in with the life of parishioners.

Churches typically anticipate that the pastor's spouse will fit in with the folk of the parish, thus serving to enhance its sense of group identity and harmony.

The alterego expectation of the parish is often unnamed and unrecognized by the parish itself. When the pastor's spouse is part of an initial interview, search committee members typically do not know what to ask (or tell) the spouse. They are not sure whether they have a right to require anything from the spouse. Yet they are extremely sensitive to vague, nonverbal impressions regarding their comfort level with the spouse. Bodies pick up vibrations and make implicit judgments about the spouse's emotional compatibility with them. Unarticulated surmises are made as to whether the spouse will accommodate to implicit rules for relating and socializing, and whether he or she will absorb the norms of parish life and respond accordingly.

Not infrequently a parish operates as if the spouse implicitly knows these rules and expectations. That assumption can lead to disastrous encounters. A new pastor's wife was asked after Thanksgiving about her plans for the children's Christmas pageant. She was startled. What pageant? She was then told that the pastor's wife was always in charge of conducting the children's Christmas Eve service. Hadn't she known that? She was shaken and outraged. From the church's perspective, however, this was a normal tradition, a way of life they had expected would continue without question; so much so that they failed to remember the need to inform, if not solicit the consent of, the spouse. Psychologically stated, the parish anticipated that the pastor's wife would be an alterego extension of their life—implicitly knowing her role, implicitly sharing the same passions and commitments, and even automatically sharing the same flow of their history. Such is the substance of which conflicts are made.

While the pastor may be expected to be an alterego for the whole parish, being an ex officio member of every church group, the spouse may get by with joining only segments of the parish self; for example, women's guild or men's group, Christian education committee, or ushering. The limited participation may be adequate for conveying a quiet "being with" the parish that contributes to its firm cohesion and smooth functioning.

Then again, a parish might split selfobject roles. The pastor, for example, may be assimilated as the idealized selfobject, while the spouse may be assimilated as the parish's alterego selfobject. This happens particularly when the idealized pastor is so awesome or revered that he or she is felt to be unapproachable, while the spouse is deemed down to earth and emotionally accessible.

Finally, the parish may implicitly expect that the spouse will be the minister's alterego, reflecting the same pastoral care and commitment as the minister who serves them. Relating to the spouse as an alterego extension of the pastor helps explain why parishioners approach the spouse in certain ways. For example, parishioners may ask the spouse about church council decisions and ecclesiastical business, as if the spouse were a partner in all the pastor knows and does. Furthermore, parishioners may tell the spouse messages to convey to the minister, as if the spouse were but another ear of the minister. Beyond this, parishioners talk to and touch the spouse as if they were touching and talking to the minister. Parishioners who are desperately afraid and lonely often reach for and squeeze the hands of ministers' wives, looking for a soothing pastoral response to keep them connected with humanity. Thus, while a spouse is not culturally considered the pastor's unpaid assistant in most parishes today, a deep tendency persists to embrace the spouse as an alterego extension of the pastor.

PART FOUR
Interpreting Conflicts

T E N
Escaping a Scalping

WHEN A COUPLE WAKES UP in the morning and begins to fight over burnt toast, the cause of the conflict is not the charred bread. Similarly, when struggles arise between pastor, spouse, and parish, the stated reason for the conflict is often not the true problem. Fixing a new slice of toast is no more an adequate solution for the couple than fixing the external complaint is for the eternal triangle. Conflict management programs employed by parishes often fail because they do not grasp the underlying needs of selves and the intense reactions of selves when they are injured.

To help us interpret the underlying meanings of struggles that occur between pastor, spouse, and parish, we will consider two stories of conflict. The one related in this chapter is about moderate struggle; the one in chapter 11 concerns severe struggle. As we said in the Introduction, by focusing on such struggles we do not imply that all is negative in pastor–spouse–parish relationships. We are simply better positioned to see the crucial role of selfobject needs in those situations where the bonds among the three are beginning to break.

HEARING THE STORY

A prominent family in Rev. Tom Palmer's parish had written a letter to the congregation stating that unless Rev. Palmer was removed from office they would withhold their contributions and withdraw from the church. Rev. Palmer had been called before the pastoral relations committee, where this and other related complaints about the conduct of his ministry were aired. The general dissatisfaction had to do with his "inability to manage his time." Not only did he spend too much time away from the church engaged in civic and denominational activities, he seemed to rush from one thing to another when at the church, meeting deadlines at the last minute and leaving matters unfinished. The result was the lack of a relaxed, competent, focused atmosphere in the church.

The Pastor Partner

Reverend Palmer was crushed. He remembered how in seminary he had vowed that he would be such a loving, caring pastor that parishioners would never be disappointed in him. It had not worked out that way. For reasons still unclear to him, he had been fired from his previous church and now stood dangerously close to being dismissed again.

Hurt soon dissolved into anger. "They have no idea what it does to a minister when he gets fired, especially when he has been hardworking and dedicated." While fearful of parish dismissal, Tom could still smile ruefully at the thought of ignorant parishioners who played underhanded games rather than confront him openly with their complaints.

He was also awed. In his words, he had "expected to be scalped," but he had not been. The church, through the pastoral relations committee, strongly suggested that he seek counseling and explicitly directed that he attend a daylong time-management course. "They saved me," he said. "They literally saved me; not just my job, but by showing some affirmation for me and getting me to look at myself." Tears came to his eyes at the good word he had received from them, which he so desperately needed—then and always.

Tom had grown up in a home where he felt disaffirmed. "I idolized my father. He was my god. I always wanted him to be proud of me, but I can't recall even one time when he did something deliberately nurturing." His father would yell at him and cuff him on the ear for his difficulty with reading, although the problem turned out to be an eye disorder. His father never attended his athletic games nor his graduations, yet was always ready to point out his son's shortcomings. While Rev. Tom Palmer's mother was generous and loved her children, the three infants who followed the first-born son in quick succession took most of her time. "I was alone a lot, and had a lot of sadness in me. I still do." He once related, with great terror, "I feel like I'm standing near a cliff, and unless I can be sure of who I am and what I have to hold on to, I'm going to be plunged over the side." As a consequence, he was always "looking for a good word" from others for everything he did in order to affirm his worth and grounding.

The parish became the primary source from which he sought this affirmation. "The church has been my first love, and my wife my second love. There's a fine line between faithful New Testament love of the church and the erotic way I see the church as a woman I love." Implicitly he assumed from the outset of their marriage that his wife would understand this.

The Clergy Spouse

Mrs. Lois Palmer did seem to understand. Although she did not like being at home alone, she complained little about Tom's frantic, consuming activities in the church. He often let family time suffer when he felt impelled to "make a call." "I realized all the pressure he had, and I saw it as my job to create a safe haven for him when he was home," she explained. That function worked well for her, for she lacked his outgoingness and ease in social situations. Her role was primarily in the home, affirming the worth of his work and taking care of him. In her own family of origin, she had also assumed the role of affirming caretaker, first for younger brothers and sisters, then for her anxiety-prone parents.

Lois Palmer's orientation toward the church followed similar lines. She implicitly expected it to be a caring body that provided affirmation for her husband and thus, through his general contentment, provided security within the home. Besides attending services with her children, she gave considerable guidance to the Christian education department of the church. She did not involve herself beyond this, however, regarding the parish as her husband's field of work.

The Congregation

St. Luke's had a compassionate nature on the whole. The previous pastor had gone through the slow, debilitating stages of Lou Gehrig's disease. It had been a difficult time for the congregation, caring and substituting for him while yearning for someone strong to care for them. Guilt kept them from asking him to leave, although his effectiveness gave out long before his body did. Prior to him they had been served by self-reliant ministers who had carried the church with their administrative guidance and pastoral care. With the coming of Rev.

Tom Palmer they had anticipated rest, renewal, and a return to pastor-centered leadership.

Although new members had joined over the years, a conservative attitude still lingered regarding the role of the minister's wife. St. Luke's could not complain about Lois Palmer's involvement because she gave such dedicated work to the Christian education department, but that did not quite match the range of activities they had anticipated she would fulfill. The parish's implicit expectations regarding a clergy's spouse were symbolically evident when they asked Lois to attend the crucial pastoral relations meeting with her husband. She was not directly criticized or questioned, but her presence had been requested as if she were her husband's intimate helper who should hear firsthand the criticisms lodged against him and the new stipulations they now had for him—or for them both.

The Growing Storm

Lois Palmer was devastated by this meeting and privately enraged. "I'll never attend another meeting like that again, ever! I was so mad that I wanted to pack up and move away that very night, and would have if we'd had a place to go." In her mind the culprit was the church, not her husband. While she continued to attend church and participate in the education program, "My heart wasn't in it like before. I felt resentful. Going there became a chore rather than something I looked forward to."

Reverend Tom Palmer's awe at being saved via the good word of the pastoral relations committee lingered with him. He somehow believed that everything was "turning out fine." After a few sessions of counseling, he announced that things were settled inside himself and with the parish. Both of these observations were inaccurate. The pastoral counselor recognized Tom Palmer's "flight into health" as his way of avoiding painful memories and vulnerabilities. In addition, a denominational official had informally contacted the pastoral counselor, explaining that the consistory president from St. Luke's had asked for assistance in dealing with Rev. Palmer, who seemed not to be taking the church matter seriously. Furthermore, the head of the pastoral relations committee had directly asked the pastoral counselor how Rev. Palmer's therapy was going, since Tom had shared nothing with them. It appeared that Rev. Palmer had not followed up on working with, and getting important feedback from, the pastoral relations committee.

As the news of continuing complaints surfaced, Tom Palmer's agitation returned. He expressed his anger at the church in his counseling sessions. At home his anger took the form of short-tempered, irritable, sarcastic responses to his wife. He had always used her as his confidant and validator, but now the intensified need for her attentiveness combined with his uncontainable frustration at the church, and his conversation with her took on a belligerent tone.

Lois bore it patiently at first, then defended herself, and then, in turn, became increasingly angry at him. She sharply rebuked his attitude, and stated at times that "no way in hell" was he going to leave for a church meeting in the middle of a family get-together. Out of anger at the church and her growing disappointment with her husband, she no longer wanted to hear his litany of complaints, nor his recital of what wonderful things he had done. While she stopped short of accusing him of causing the problems in the parish, she began to be direct in her criticism of his behavior at home. As stress generated more stress, Tom Palmer began to contemplate divorce. "It seemed to me that the only way to get some peace in my life was to leave her."

INTERPRETING THE DRAMA

Each self felt painfully injured. Anger and hopelessness surfaced as cherished expectations about how other would respond were dashed. The resulting signs of fragmentation were clear.

Threatened Self-Cohesion

Reverend Tom Palmer regressed into self-pity, enraged blame, and disavowal of difficulties. He contemplated unrealistic solutions such as divorcing the "second love" of his life. Lois Palmer's loss of self-cohesion was evident in her emotional withdrawal from the church, her withdrawal of support from her husband, and her regressive lapse into uncharacteristic behavior (swearing and frustrated criticism). St. Luke's disintegration was shown in its protective, circumscribed, reactionary thinking (that the problem was the pastor's) and in its splintered, divisive action (single parishioners trying to dictate community decisions; the consistory bypassing and failing to inform the pastor when denominational officials were being contacted; the pastoral relations committee personnel soliciting private information from Rev. Palmer's counselor without the pastor's knowledge or consent).

And yet each self managed to retain sufficient self-cohesion to allow for continuation of their relationships. In quieter moments of restored self-esteem, Tom Palmer could recognize that his divorce thoughts were desperate, unwanted plans. He was able to contemplate the legitimacy of St. Luke's dissatisfactions with him and began to have an inkling of the defensive nature of his "all is fine" attitude.

Lois Palmer's self-cohesion did not totally collapse either. While her involvement in the church was devitalized, she did not abandon her work there. Neither did she vent her anger at the church directly, or covertly seek revenge. She also remained committed to her marriage. Her rage at her husband boiled over at times, but for the most part it was metered out in proportion to his irrationality.

For all of St. Luke's feelings of disillusionment and abandonment, it was still able to extend support to its pastor, to give him a second chance, and to appropriately deal with the tension created by certain parishioners who demanded the pastor's instant resignation. None-theless, marital and parish relationships were significantly strained.

Frustrated Selfobject Needs

Reverend Tom Palmer was motivated by chronic needs for mirroring acclaim. The "good word" that never came from his criticism-laden father or his busy mother left a profound emptiness inside him. He was always dependent on an affirming word to bolster his self-esteem and to keep him from his cliff of despair. Understandably he was also vigilant for disconfirming responses. "I'm very fragile. I always want to feel there's nothing I can't do and nothing I can't do well. When people criticize me or don't go along with my plans, I get anxious and defensive." When under increased disaffirming pressures, he would deny there was any problem at all, or compensate with fantasies of how great he was doing.

The parish was Tom Palmer's primary mirroring selfobject. Lois Palmer was his secondary mirroring selfobject. From both he expected a natural, uninterrupted flow of mirroring responses. He was not naive about this. He knew criticisms were inevitable. But in his inner self, that child part of him still yearned for applauding responses—and expected them. In his mind he would be the loving pastor whom everyone would always affirm. When that mirroring affirmation was not forthcoming, he was shocked and angered.

Lois Palmer operated out of a need for a security-creating, idealized selfobject. Tom Palmer was her central soothing source, whose strength and competence she expected would create an environment of constancy and well-being for her. Her previous caretaking roles with siblings and parents had not made her firmly self-reliant. What she missed was the presence of a person whose strength and care she could incorporate and make her own. Consequently, she still reached out for individuals who could provide steady security for her. As she provided affirming care now for her husband, she inwardly anticipated that he would be empowered to care for her.

The marriage of Tom and Lois Palmer was formed around an interfacing of mirroring-idealizing needs. The principal marriage dance by which they attempted to get these needs met was the dance of collusion. She would tolerate being a second to his primary love (the church), would sacrifice family and personal times for his needs to shine, and would be constantly affirming of his work. In return he was to provide a protective, secure environment that she could count on to help her feel inwardly safe. He, in turn, acted strong and even self-righteously condescending so that she, in her dependent, self-giving way, would continue to be a secret support for his often sagging self-esteem.

Not coincidentally, Rev. Palmer attempted to establish the same colluding relationship with the parish. He implicitly assumed that St. Luke's would tolerate his out-of-church activities, just as his wife tolerated his out-of-home activities. Moreover, he implicitly expected that St. Luke's would continue to affirm him no matter what, just as his affirming caretaker wife did. When difficulties surfaced with St. Luke's, he minimized (disavowed) the trouble, just as he did with his wife's complaints.

But St. Luke's would have nothing of the collusion he wanted to create with them. They looked for a strong leader, one who would be the center of initiative and pastoral nurturing for the church. In so doing, the pastor would fulfill the idealized ministerial role they had been familiar with in the past, and would compensate for the strain of role reversal experienced with the previous minister, who had left them with the burden of self-guidance and self-sustainment.

When the pastor's mirroring expectations and the parish's idealizing expectations became increasingly thwarted, the collusional relationship between pastor and spouse was disrupted. Collusion then gave way to contending. Tom Palmer became deidealized by his wife to a degree, and Lois Palmer became devalued as a mirroring support by her husband to a degree. The degree was great enough, especially in light of their vulnerable self-cohesion, to cause a significant stress in their marriage. Fortunately their relationship did not totally disintegrate. While periods of contemplated divestment occurred, these were transitory.

We see in this triangular relationship how disruptions in one part of the triangle can result in disruptions in its other parts. Thus, the refusal of St. Luke's to respond as a colluding, mirroring selfobject for Rev. Palmer's weakly structured self precipitated his intensified need for mirroring from his wife and his regressive use of her as an outlet for his rage at the church. One central theme throughout these chapters has been that when pastors or spouses experience being injured by the parish, this injury contributes to, if not provokes, difficulties between the clergy couple. What is new in all this is the particular way of understanding and interpreting the needs, injuries, and reactions of all the selves involved.

Restorations

The same interpretative insights can help us understand how changes in one part of the eternal triangle can promote healing in all relationships. Rev. Palmer, for instance, was crushed by the failure of St. Luke's to function as a beneficently admiring selfobject, but he was also genuinely awed that they had "saved" him. He was deeply touched by this—not just after the first meeting when he found out he was not being terminated, but even months later. Simultaneous with his initial and periodic rage at St. Luke's for failing to affirm him, and simultaneous with the displacement of his anger upon his wife, he also felt a counteracting gratitude that held the potential for his feeling redeemed and for his marriage to be healed. We will look at the healthy consequences first and then go back to interpret them.

Several months after the infamous pastoral relations meeting, Rev. Palmer made this somewhat startling statement: "I realize that I have to do something with this church that I have been unwilling to do with it and other churches I've served. I have to learn about its personality and join with it. And I want to do that now. I feel more and more that I'm a 'belonger.' " He then related, almost in the same breath, "The story of the prodigal son has always moved me to tears, especially the ending. I have forever wanted to experience that with my father, the embrace that says I'm OK." In addition to his softened approach to the church and his emerging awareness of a profound yearning for his father's affirmation, he also expressed feeling more connected to

Lois Palmer. "I am deeply moved by her long-suffering with me, and by her caretaking that I can never match nor ever repay."

Reverend Tom Palmer's warm empathy and tender desire for intimacy are movingly evident here. But what brought about this stabilization and expansion of his self? What happened to bring him back from a fractured, bitter state to one of compassion and renewed hope? The constant support of his pastoral counselor was a crucial factor in helping him regain his equilibrium. The refusal of his wife to give up on him, or to blame him for St. Luke's complaints, helped restore him to his rightful mind.

Just as important was a profound experience with his "first love," the church. He felt saved by the church, not only in terms of employment but in terms of his whole self. The church's affirmation and embrace of him in the midst of his shortcomings was like that redeeming fatherly hug he had so yearned for. The deep-in-the-soul assurances of his worth that he so desperately missed from his father, and that he so painfully envied in the prodigal son story, now became a subjective reality for him as his mirroring selfobject church recognized his errors and yet opened its arms to him. One part of him was crushed, as the old experiences of his father's revilements were heard again in the church's criticism. But simultaneously he also "heard the good word," experienced profoundly the wedding of criticism with affirmation, and he felt saved. An empathic act by the parish set in motion a process of restoration. In the nourishing warmth of a sensitive response, he was made sufficiently whole to look anew at himself and to begin changing the definitions and boundaries of his life. Churches can also be blessings for pastors and their marriages.

CLARIFYING THE PLOTS

This story of one eternal triangle illustrates that when pastors, spouses, and congregations lack an understanding of the selfobject issues at work between them, they typically attempt to work out their struggles by focusing on organizational issues. Rev. Tom Palmer, Lois Palmer, and St. Luke's recognized there were powerful influences afoot, but in an effort to manage the conflict (i.e., to assuage the anxiety that such conflict generates), they tended to reduce the problem by making it one of time. St. Luke's complained to Rev. Palmer and to denominational officials about the pastor's lack of time at the church. Rev. Palmer complained that the church often wanted too much time. Lois

Palmer began to set boundaries in the deteriorating marriage by demanding that Tom Palmer "keep family time family time."

But time itself was not the problem; it was what time meant psychologically to the self of each that was crucial. Time for St. Luke's really meant the soothing, guiding comfort of an indwelling, receptive pastor (a doctoring, directing, idealized selfobject). Time for Rev. Palmer meant the granted freedom to move from group to group in order to receive doses of affirmation he needed to keep the core of his self cohesive (a need for worth-giving mirroring responses). Time for Lois Palmer meant a symbolic assurance of constancy, of an intact, nonfragmenting environment in which she could maintain her own emotional equilibrium (a need for a security-generating idealized selfobject). Simply accommodating to the time demands of the other, however, would not have necessarily led to any change in the underlying relationships. Any adequate resolution of this struggle between pastor, spouse, and parish would require deeper understandings and interpretations regarding time.

Finally, it is appropriate to acknowledge that tolerance is a virtue in many eternal triangles. Many Protestant churches give inefficiently functioning ministers repeated chances to change before imposing serious reprisals. Many pastors give narrow-spirited parishes uncounted opportunities to grow before calling in outside forces or leaving. And many clergy couples bless their partners with steadfast love that endures all things. For these capacities we must give thanks.

ELEVEN
Lacking Arms and Glue

A N OLD APHORISM SAYS that it does not matter where we go or what we do or how much we have, it is who we have beside us that counts. When no arms embrace us and we have little emotional glue to keep us feeling connected to others, then we are extremely vulnerable to despair. In this next story we meet a pastor, clergy spouse, and parish in a more fragmented condition than Rev. Tom Palmer, Lois Palmer, and St. Luke's. This story illustrates severe individual self-difficulties, desperate reliance upon others for emotional stability, and indomitable, in many ways courageous, efforts to keep the self together. Moreover, it briefly points up a frequent but unrecognized self-state in many churches, namely a state of mourning.

HEARING THE STORY

Reverend Dan and Mrs. Julie Weber were fighting. She accused him of being unreliable, of thinking only of his own needs, and of not being able to stand up to the church. Most often he had responded with chilly silence. Recently, however, he found himself pulling the car off to the side of the road and yelling at her. She was not supportive of him, he blasted. Not only did she refuse his sexual needs, she also refused his need of her presence in church. He wanted her in the worship service while he preached, but she was forever finding some excuse for not being there. Her absence was making his relationship with the congregation even more difficult. In the face of his barrages, she began to withdraw into herself.

Each felt agonizingly alone. There was no one either of them could turn to for embracing arms or an encouraging word. Certainly not each other. Their outbursts and silent treatments had caused a severe deterioration in their relationship. They withheld the comforting responses from each other that they so vitally needed. The more intense and frequent the fighting became, the more each worried about falling apart, as a person and as a couple.

The Clergy Spouse

In this present condition, Julie Weber could tolerate only minimal contact with her husband. "Hold me if you need to but without any demands," she would say to Dan. "I'm doing all I can to hold myself together. Don't expect anything from me. I can't stand that."

His requests that she come to church enraged her. She did not want to hear him preach. She did not even want to go into the church. "I feel that if I sit down in the pews, I'll start screaming right in the middle of the service." She suffered from constant headaches and stomach disturbances that no medication could alleviate.

As a child, Julie had been sexually abused by a stepfather and left unprotected by her mother. She felt both betrayed and abandoned. Deep feelings of apprehension filled her. Nothing ever seemed certain. Good experiences failed to last, being shattered by current worries or past remembrances. Avoidance of injury rather than pursuit of joy became every day's project. And yet she longed to be connected to someone or something she could experience as dependable, predictable, and reliable.

She now despaired of finding that in her husband. He could not be counted on. He was preoccupied with the church. When he promised to be home, he was always late, always with an elaborate, well-justified excuse. When he was home, and promised to watch their infant son, he would become so engrossed in his own activities that he came close to what she considered negligence. When he promised to be more sensitive to her needs and feelings, he quickly forgot. She felt betrayed and abandoned again, let down by him as she sensed being let down by so many other significant people in her life.

The Pastor Partner

By contrast, Rev. Dan Weber was frantically involved in parish activity. No matter how much effort he put in, however, the church did not respond. Nothing seemed to be enough. Unable to detect where the problem lay, he assumed it was his fault. Lacking any idea of how to change the situation, he simply worked harder and harder at what he was already doing.

His ministry felt empty as well as futile. His pastoral acts, for example, seemed detached from him as a person, as if he were just acting. Proclaiming the faith felt like recitation, saying what he should say. He felt that he neither possessed the skills the pastoral role called for nor embodied the faith he was to rehearse for others. Indeed, he was not sure what he believed or what he really wanted.

Dan had grown up in a religious home. His parents were steady but emotionally restrictive. Harmony at home was everything. The expression of negative or angry feelings was discouraged, with mother citing scripture verses admonishing peace and forgiveness. Appearance was everything, too. His mother's frequent phrase was, "Be as good as you look." His folks' comments on his preaching later in life remained consistent with this latter theme. They would say, "You looked and sounded good today."

Mother and father's minds "filled the room," leaving little space for his own feelings and thoughts to emerge. As long as he fulfilled their expectations regarding his spiritual duty and social behavior, he felt the security of their goodwill. To deviate from family norms, however, meant subtle but painful rebuff. Even into his adult life, he twinged at the thought of being reduced to a passing reference in the last paragraph of his parents' annual Christmas newsletter after having disappointed them.

As a result, Dan Weber developed into what he called a people pleaser. He had difficulty getting in touch with his own feelings or knowing what he really believed. He knew how to accommodate others, to keep the peace, but he had little conception of what it meant to nourish others, to be with others on a sustained emotional basis. At the same time, he had trouble setting boundaries, often failing to discern inappropriateness and potential danger in relationships with others. "Nothing really feels like it's under my control," he said. "It's hard to give direction to the church when I feel inwardly directionless, not knowing what I want or think is important. And it's hard to keep consistent with my promises to my wife when I don't feel consistent inside myself."

When the denomination assigned Rev. Dan Weber to Grace Church after his ordination, both he and his wife were filled with high hopes. The parish was located in a rural area of a western state. Both had grown up in the Midwest, and the prospect of moving to a different area and of starting a ministry career signaled new beginnings for them. Those expectations were soon crushed.

The Congregation

Grace Church was politically conservative, theologically narrow, and emotionally closed. An ingrown sense of "we-ness" prevailed, along with a suspiciousness about strangers. The parish kept mostly to itself as a congregation, using its facilities for its own activities while rejecting requests by civil and social groups to meet in its building.

One sign of Grace's circumscribed inclusiveness, as well as of its rejection of Rev. Weber's efforts, came in a criticism inserted into the church newsletter by the church president: "I have heard comments that some people don't like to read the pastor's articles, that our newsletter doesn't have enough stuff in it about the personal lives of our members, like columns in local newspapers which used to report on 'What's Happening in Brookfield Township.' "

That subtle "we-and-them" attitude operated with potentially new church members as well. A nearby housing development brought new faces to visit the church, but strangers seldom joined. As one perceptive parishioner stated, "If a person does become a new member here and gets involved, he's going to be a good member, because you have to go through a lot to be accepted here."

Reverend Dan Weber and Julie Weber fared no better than other new faces. Rev. Weber had a position in the church but no place; that is, he was accepted formally as the leader of the church but not embraced socially or emotionally. Julie Weber also had a position, namely "pastor's wife," but also no place. She was always referred to formally, "Mrs. Weber," or in the third person, "the pastor's wife." There was no extended community of warmth or invitation. Except for church functions, Dan and Julie Weber had no other contact with parish members.

To make matters worse, Dan and Julie were forever hearing how wonderful the previous pastor and his wife had been. The parish's repeated theme was how well that couple had fit in with the congregation and what a wonderful job they had done. Conversation about them and pictures of them still circulated. It was enough to make Julie want to scream right in the middle of the service, for not only were these impossible models to compete with, but both she and her husband had experienced no significantly caring responses from the congregation at all. "I thought that when I finally had a baby, then people would come around and warm up, but they never did," agonized the young mother. Recalled Rev. Weber, "When we came, I was told that Grace Church had no financial problems and wouldn't if I did my job. Then when we had money problems, I blamed myself, only to find out later that the church had financial problems before I came. But the message was that it was my job and responsibility alone."

INTERPRETING THE DRAMA

Dan and Julie Weber were severely fragmented. This loss of essential self-cohesion was evident in Julie Weber's incapacity to enjoy or endure physical contact, in her depressive withdrawal, and in the psychosomatic disturbances she suffered. Signs that the smooth functioning of Rev. Weber's self had been lost were his obsessively driven behavior, his depersonalization experiences (feeling detached from his work and his own words), and his impaired ability for reality-testing in human relationships. Both individuals had come into the marriage, and to the position at Grace Church, with weakly structured selves.

Traumatized Selfobject World

As a child, Julie Weber's parental selfobjects were not merely insufficient, they were actively traumatizing. The trauma, however, was not primarily to her body but to her self. At the deepest level, the violation of her unprotected body was a violation of the core of her young being. What she had needed as a child were idealized parents, parents who acted with comforting reliability so that she could develop assured feelings of being surrounded by a predictable world. She had needed her parents to be dependable, so that inner feelings of being surrounded by a supportive world could become part of her outlook on life.

The reality of her parents became the condition of her self. The severe failure of her selfobject parents became the severe fragility of her self. Her unreliable and undependable parental world became her inner world of insecurity and vigilance. The psychological effort of her self became nothing more complex than simply protecting the fragile remnant of self she still clung to.

Tentatively, therefore, she came into the marriage hoping to find an idealized substitute, one who would be tolerantly undemanding (nonthreatening to her vulnerable self), protectively alert (helping to ward off potential threats to her self), and soothingly reliable and dependable (compensating for her parents' failures). Her emotional needs were deep, her expectations excessive. She required and demanded near-perfect responses from her husband in order to feel safe inside. Dan Weber failed at this, both because of normal limitations as a human being and because of his pronounced personal difficulties. As a result, Julie Weber became enraged and disillusioned. She withdrew emotionally, sexually, and as a clergy spouse. These actions were part of her contending with him, an assertive, panic-driven effort to wrench from him the promises he had made, which she took not just as promises for meeting daily duties but as promises for her self's salvation.

While her self-protecting efforts may have cut her off from possibilities for new, healing relationships, her efforts must also be seen as health promoting. Safeguarding her emotional core was psychologically her ultimate purpose, as it is for all of us. She was in a necessary survival mode, given how she experienced her situation. However regressive or childish her self-protective efforts might appear, they were her way of trying to get on with her life, to find that sense of inner peace she so desperately desired.

Precarious Self-Cohesion

Dan Weber's parental selfobjects were sufficiently reliable and dependable. As a result, the core of his self, unlike his wife's, was not always on the verge of disintegration. But the support for his self-cohesion was always narrowly and precariously based. He could maintain an inner state of well-being only as long as he felt incorporated into and in sync with his powerful parents. By pleasing them through meeting their expectations, he felt assured of being comfortingly included by them and blessed by them. Accommodating to their prescriptions and requirements gave a steady direction to his life. Molding his self to the world of his idealized parents promised the prize of their goodwill, and thus the possibility of his feeling inwardly secure.

Within his family, to be self-assertive and demand his own way was to court his parents' disapproval. Rebellion against their expectations opened the possibility of being chastened, isolated, and left on his own. As a result, he was unable to develop the ability to know his own feelings and thoughts and to act on them. He was unable to develop the capacity to understand other people's motives and needs and to stand up for himself when necessary. His only method for maintaining internal well-being was to stay safely connected to definition-giving, reality-instructing others. Consequently, Dan Weber as a boy and young man remained bound to his parents, taking his shape from them and being soothed by the approval his pleasing behavior could elicit from them. By his accommodating behavior and frantic labor he abandoned his self to similarly powerful individuals throughout his life. In so doing he avoided falling apart, but at the price of genuine creativity and authenticity.

Supportive responses from others are necessary for the development of a person's capacities for self-direction, self-motivation, and self-reflection. Dan Weber had needed emotionally flexible idealized parental figures who could have lent their strength and encouragement to their son in the process of his finding his own way. But rather than standing as nonthreatened and nonthreatening parents who allowed their son to establish his own separate identity and internal self-confidence, they demanded his compliance to their chosen way. He was to function as their selfobject instead of they as his. However well-intended, they absorbed their son into their world, leaving him with limited capacities for self-monitoring and initiative.

Reverend Dan Weber came into his marriage expecting his wife to function as his supportive idealized selfobject. "I made her my emotional center," he said later. More explicitly, he relied upon her to fill in for his inadequately developed capacities. For instance, she was expected to be his "eyes and ears." Unadept at picking up emotional clues from others and fathoming what was going on in relationships, he relied upon her ultrasensitive radar to keep him informed. Limited in the ability to give direction to his life and work, he elicited her suggestions for appropriate action in certain situations. Deficient in the ability to soothe himself, he relied upon her to reduce his tension. She was expected, in this regard, to give herself to him sexually as a means of assuaging his general distress. Moreover, he needed the sight of her face in church when he fearfully entered the pulpit, for there, more than at any other place, he stood vulnerable to criticism. Like a child in a school play anxiously scanning the audience to see if mother is comfortingly there, he searched for her presence to fortify his quaking spirit. Dan Weber psychologically embraced his wife as an idealized selfobject, whose soothing presence was his emotional center, and whose perceptive skills he depended upon for successful satisfaction of others' demands upon him.

Using his wife to keep him personally and ecclesiastically afloat had nothing of growth in it. Dan Weber was not borrowing some of Julie Weber's capacities in order to learn them for himself. He was banking on them to be there over and over again for him to draw on. Rather than incorporating her skills for his own personal growth, he merely used them for satisfying his external world, upon which his own sense of security was based. When Julie Weber failed in her role, he reacted first with passive aggression (cold, distancing behavior), and then, when his life in the parish began to collapse, with overt attacks. The Weber marriage was formed around an interfacing of the idealizing needs of both partners. The principal marriage dance by which they attempted to have these needs met was one of contention.

Both Rev. Dan Weber and Julie Weber came to Grace Church with intense idealizing needs. For Dan Weber, the parish was to be an emotional extension of his parents, a substitute idealized selfobject in the form of a community. For Julie Weber, the church was to be an emotional replacement for her parents, a compensating idealized self-object in the form of a community. Her yearnings for the church were touchingly evident in a note to a friend before going to Grace: "My husband and I are far from being intimate. I know we have a lot of work and struggles ahead. Pray that we find support in our new community."

Circumscribed Alterego

Grace Church, however, was disinclined to meet their needs. In the first place, the parish was an alterego community with long-standing, implicit criteria for emotional and social inclusion. Although not an ethnically oriented church, it still functioned as one. A cultural mentality of "we-ness" prevailed, based not only upon a history of theological and political conservatism, but also upon a geographical inbredness that made it suspicious of outsiders.

The circumscribed alterego life of Grace Church made it difficult for the parish to warmly welcome its new pastor and his wife. It could allow formal inclusion, allowing the Webers to play their roles as pastor and pastor's wife, but could not extend itself to include them personally. Grace Church was ill equipped, therefore, to meet the idealization needs of the couple.

Grace Church was also ill disposed to meet these needs. As a group self it was going through its own pain. Grace had not yet worked through its mourning over the loss of its beloved, former alterego clergy couple. The church still maintained a fantasized presence of the former couple through repeated reminiscences and rehearsals about them, and so maintained a feeling of continued belonging to and longing for them. Consequently, there was a lack of emotional space for Dan and Julie Weber.

Moreover, Grace's nonresponsiveness to Rev. Dan Weber's ministry and its general distancing from the Webers as a couple were expressions of hostility toward the interlopers. Just as children often react with rejecting hostility toward a new mother or father brought into the blended home to replace a beloved lost parent, so too did Grace Church react negatively toward the new clergy couple who came to supplant their beloved alterego clergy couple. Dan and Julie Weber were not family.

As Rev. Weber became increasingly panicked over not being able to satisfy Grace Church (his parentified idealized selfobject community), his self-cohesion began to fragment. He thus became increasingly insistent that Julie Weber (his function-enhancing idealized selfobject partner) fortify his work and assuage his stress. As Julie Weber became increasingly upset with her husband (her reliability-assuring idealized selfobject partner) and increasingly disillusioned with the parish (her replacement idealized selfobject community), she divested energy from the latter and turned evermore contendingly toward the former for attentiveness and support. Her divestment from the church and intensified demands on her husband intensified his anxieties (he had limited internal resources for self-reflection and self-soothing), which led to his regressive contendings with her and his increased obsessive activities with the parish. This behavior on his part left her feeling more abandoned and betrayed. As selfobject failure mounted on selfobject failure, the selves of Dan and Julie Weber began to severely disintegrate, along with that hope-filled embrace they once called their marriage.

CLARIFYING THE PLOTS

In this eternal triangle we once again see how the selves of pastor, spouse, and congregation impact upon each other. Many pastors with self-difficulties are able to function adequately as ministers as long as their marriages help them maintain emotional equilibrium—often, however, at tremendous emotional cost for the spouse. When both spouse and pastor struggle with each other for assurances and the pastor's equilibrium is not maintained via the marriage, both marriage and ministry break down. That occurred in the case of the Webers.

Correspondingly, many pastors with self-difficulties are able to function adequately as marriage partners as long as their parishes help them maintain a sense of well-being. When that self-preserving relationship with the church is lost, both ministry and marriage tend to break down. That occurred in the case of the Palmers in the last chapter.

Then again, many clergy spouses with self-difficulties are able to function as adequate marriage partners, and to be satisfied with being the spouse of a minister, as long as their selfobject pastor partner experiences personal fulfillment in the ministry and is able to handle interpersonal relationships in the congregation adequately. When parish dissent arises, disturbing the smooth internal workings of the pastor's self, the spouse's cohesion in both marriage and ministry is threatened.

This present case illustrates, especially in the person of Rev. Weber, how a vulnerable self accommodates to whatever the primary selfobjects have to offer. Many ministers and spouses remain in debilitating parishes and in degrading marriages because of their dependence on what they consider indispensable selfobjects. They are like children who will mold themselves to the demands of their omnipotently perceived, life-determining mothers or fathers in order to receive some token of recognition and care. Parishes may do the same with omnipotently perceived pastors. A depth understanding of these self-dynamics helps us to respond with empathy rather than with moralizations.

Congregational Mourning

Pastors, spouses, and parishes have emotional agendas of which they are often not aware. Grace Church was in a self-state we commonly call mourning. More churches are in some stage of grief than we realize—grief that is not only masked from awareness, but whose external manifestations are disavowed as grief.

While other factors were involved, the negativity shown by Grace Church toward the Webers was part of its mourning over the loss of its former alterego clergy couple. This negativity protected the memory and sense of presence of the former alterego couple, which the parish self at that time needed for the maintenance of its self-cohesion.

The parish's negativity during this vulnerable time was also a self-protective defense against once again being disillusioned (left) by a new (hoped-for) selfobject clergy couple. Keeping the new couple at a distance minimized the possibility of once again being hurt, an injury that could bring further fragmentation to Grace's vulnerable state of being. The process of grief and mourning takes on greater meaning when understood as the self's response to loss of crucial selfobjects.

Misplaced Interpretations

Finally, although Rev. Dan Weber, Julie Weber, and Grace Church did not attribute their relationship troubles to time difficulties as Rev. Tom Palmer, Lois Palmer, and St. Luke's were inclined to do, time in the above scenario could once again be promoted—inappropriately—as a central factor in the rise of stress. It is commonly interpreted, for example, that too much time in the pastorate and too much time in a current position lead to clergy burnout. Conversely, it is commonly posited that shortness of time in the pastorate and shortness of time in a current position significantly increase the chances of emotional problems. Consequently it might be claimed that the Webers' difficulties in the parish emerged in part because they were "green" in the ministry and new to Grace Church. Had they been buttressed by years of pastoral activity, they might have managed the situation better, both personally and professionally.

While there may be various peaks of stress in ministry, these should not be attributed to time issues but to self issues. Time in the ministry has nothing directly to do with personal or professional maturity. Some ministers with thirty years of service repeatedly establish debilitating relationships from church to church. Some novice preachers, from the first, minister with healthy self-esteem and mature regard for others. Time in the ministry reflects one's state of self, rather than one's state of self reflecting time in the ministry.

Just as time is not a cause of problems, neither does time heal pastor, spouse, or parish wounds. Persons are healed as they feel embraced by empathic selfobject individuals. Time is not a selfobject, although some persons might be soothed by the thought of having "time on their side." Time becomes an instant but trivialized interpretation when confusion and complexity assail us, much like our knee-jerk interpretation of "God's will" when tragedy strikes and we cannot bear its meaninglessness. The harder but more productive effort lies in acknowledging selfobject needs in ourselves and others, and how we all respond with varying degrees of rage and withdrawal when our selfobjects fail us—as they inevitably do.

Objective situations (for example, church size, whether the clergy spouse is employed or unemployed, denominational polity, theological orientation, amount of money earned) do not adequately predict vocational satisfaction and commitment, either to ministry in general or to a particular parish. What determines a sense of fulfillment and the ability to run the good race of ministry are the pastor's subjective feelings. The internal subjective viewpoint of the self, who experiences the world primarily as selfobjects, shapes commitment and satisfaction. This helps explain, once again, why some ministers who are objectively successful feel internally empty, while others who struggle with church work live life with vigorous enthusiasm.

PART FIVE
Reaching Out for Help

TWELVE
Gift Getting

A FRIEND OF MINE in the ministry still reminds me, "God's spirit will empower if the minister gets out of the way." He tells the story of a guest preacher who was startled to see a brass plate on the inside of the pulpit that read, "Sir, we would see Jesus." That is a backdoor way of saying that ministers will bear good fruit if they just keep Christ central in their lives. I believe that. I take that thought with me into every counseling session with a pastor or clergy couple, and into every consultation on parish problems. My inner prayer is that God's spirit will be in the room, guiding, correcting, healing.

I utter that same prayer now as we enter into these final chapters. As we talk of primary ways pastors, spouses, and parishes can reach for health and wholeness, we affirm our ultimate reliance upon God's healing power. May the following suggestions for the maintenance and restoration of selves be "of God." For their inevitable limitations, we ask God's fulfillment. For any errors, we ask God's forgiveness.

ADDITIVE MISTAKES

"Why do men chase women?" the pastor's wife asked, a few weeks after urinating on her husband's favorite jacket after discovering his affairs (see chapter 6). "Men chase women when they're afraid of dying," she finally concluded. Armed with that conviction, she waited up for him late one night. When he entered the door she screamed: "Listen! Listen to me! You're going to die, just like everyone else. You hear me? You're going to die!"[15]

An author writing about clergy marriages expounded on how the "hungry ego" of pastor and spouse often takes "center stage." Each partner puts his or her self first, giving in to selfish "egocentricism." What is needed, suggested the author, is an "act of will," a committed decision to relinquish one's hungry ego in favor of marital nurturance and growth.

Mistakes are additive. Although the wrathful wife's attempt to slap her husband into reality is understandable, it had little effect. Indeed, frustration-filled remedies of pastors, spouses, and parishes often increase the very loneliness they are trying to overcome. Although writers may be genuinely concerned about inward spiritual decay, flaws in their articles on ministers, spouses, and congregations combine into cumulative misleading analyses of problems and solutions. Personal and professional interpretations may be traveling down the right road in the right direction, but unfortunately in the wrong lane.

On the other hand, common sense and compassion are not enough for pastors, spouses, and parishes in trouble. Relationships in the eternal triangle are more complicated than most of us have believed. Many emotional injuries can be averted, however, and current injuries healed, by a broadened understanding of the needs of the self. The following chapters highlight the essential ingredients necessary for being and staying a healthy self.

A HEALTHY SELF

Pastors, spouses, and parishes regain the joy of work, the inspiration of ideals, and the assurance of belonging as they: (1) receive nurturing responses from others, (2) possess a deep understanding as to why those responses are so important, and (3) give their selves to others in supportive ways.

What, for example, were the immediate responses that Rev. Janice and Mr. Charles Talbot needed in order to preserve their self-cohesion and to move them toward regained feelings of well-being? They first needed to receive empathic responses. Charles needed concrete affirming acts from his wife. He needed to have a word of endearment whispered in his ear, to be fondly touched, to be looked at longingly. Janice needed concrete soothing acts from her husband. She needed an arm around her shoulder, a calming smile, a word of promise from him to stand by her. Both yearned for the other to really understand them and to respond accordingly.

In my response to Charles I attempted to express a resonating understanding of his pain, anger, and longing. As he sensed that someone understood him, was attuned to the truth of his statements and actions, his rage receded a bit, and hope began to return. My response was also a low-level interpretation. That interpretation was later combined with more complete interpretations regarding his reliance on selfobject figures and his rage when they did not meet his expectations. As he and Janice began to empathically understand what was happening, that is, to mentally grasp the meaning of their wounds and the workings of their selves, they were better able to soothe themselves when upset and to be more tolerant of each other when they felt injured.

Finally, Janice and Charles experienced renewed joy in life and commitment to values as they more fully responded empathically to others. Mirroring others, allowing others to idealize them, and acting as alterego companions filled them with quiet pride. As they did unto others as others had done unto them, they felt themselves embodying their faith more honestly and united more intimately with beloved care-givers. They regained self-cohesion by being empathic selfobjects for others—including one another.

In summary, pastors, clergy spouses, and parishes feel renewed inner life when they feel securely connected to special people upon whom they can rely to help them hold their selves together. Healing does not come when we are slapped in the face with reality, nor when we are exhorted to acts of will. Healing occurs when individuals and congregations are empathically affirmed, soothed, and accepted. Healing comes when we feel the empathic support of another, who gives his or her self to us in such a way that we feel that person is a part of us. Only then may the slapping or exhorting remedies have some effective power.

Members of the eternal triangle are also renewed, and their relationship strengthened, as they gain a new understanding of what motivates them to act and react as they do. As they come to possess illuminating explanations and interpretations, they are better able to hold their selves together and to develop tolerance and concern for others.

Finally, pastors, spouses, and parishes become more of what they were created to be as they practice hospitality, that is, as they respond to others in empathic, caring ways. We become healed when we act in healing ways.

Getting the Needed Responses

When a pastor, spouse, or congregation responds to us in a thoughtful way, we are often filled with gratitude. Indeed, for those of us who believe God's spirit works in all things for good, we give thanks for this manifestation of divine grace. An attitude of humility is quite proper.

But we do not need to think that in this process of receiving empathic responses we should stand as waiting, passive recipients. A theme throughout these pages has been that it is healthy for us to actively attempt to evoke supportive responses from others. Attempting to elicit mirroring, idealizing, or alterego responses is normal, even though it is often done in archaic, immature ways. Seeking empathic, sustaining responses is part of the maintenance of health for a pastor, spouse, or parish. Even overdone efforts are to be appreciated, for they are desperate attempts by persons or parishes to protect their vulnerable inner core.

A pastor is capable of changing her self or his self so as to create new opportunities for receiving supportive responses. A clergy spouse can actively influence his or her selfobject figures in assertive, helpful ways. A parish can try again even in the face of disappointments, looking for new ways to get needs met. Difficulties arise in part for pastors, spouses, and parishes when they fail to seek out and evoke empathic selfobject responses.

When pastors enter into the pulpit, therefore, it is healthy for them to present their selves in ways that elicit mirroring responses from parishioners. Historically, pastors have focused so much on their sinful, "hungry ego's" demand for the limelight that they have underemphasized the appropriate desire to feel exalted in the very act of doing God's work. They have likewise passed over the possibility that accolades from preaching can be a means of grace for the pastor's own healing and restoration.

When spouses enter into the parish, it is healthy for them to actively make themselves available for alterego companionship. They have worried so much about not showing partiality that they have neglected their appropriate need to be connected intimately to particular parishioners. Furthermore, it is healthy for them to seek out idealized pastors other than their partner. They have felt so obliged to be "a good supportive spouse" that they have ignored their spiritual needs for their own inspiring minister.

When we enter into our bedrooms, it is healthy for us to present our selves in physical-romantic ways that elicit our spouse's admiring responses. Likewise, it is healthy to coax comfort from our spouse, or to invite our spouse to feel and think like we do for a while.

When parishes enter into relationship with a new pastor and spouse, it is healthy for them to put their best foot forward in anticipation of being praised and affirmed. Similarly, a parish creates potentials for empathic responses by fostering confidence in the very pastor and spouse from whom it looks to draw strength, and by reinforcing important similarities between the clergy couple and itself.

These actions are not manipulative; they are not examples of a narcissistic generation. They are as normal as asking for a hug, and as much a blessing for the hugger as for the "huggee."

Using the Responses Given

An old story tells of a man on the roof of his flooded house. As the water rose, a neighbor in a canoe came to help him. "No thanks," he replied. "God will save me." As the water rose higher, a rescuer in a rowboat arrived to take him to safety. "No need," he stated. "God will save me." Finally, with the water washing over the roof's peak, a motorboat sped up. "It's all right," he shouted back. "God will save me." Soon after that the waters engulfed him and he drowned. When he came face to face with God, he was angry. "I trusted you. I believed you would save me but you let me down." "What do you mean?" replied God. "I sent a boat for you three times."

Often we dismiss empathic responses as not powerful enough to save us, when in themselves they may well be the answer to our prayers for help. The problem at times is not the unavailability of empathic responses, but our unwillingness to stoop to accept them.

Part of preserving our spirit is relying upon the common, everyday empathic gestures of others. They come from the elderly ladies who shake the pastor's hand every Sunday and say the same appreciative words. They come from the spouse who may not have much to say about a sermon except "It went well today." For the parish they come from the pastor's calm manner and from the spouse's smile and warm laughter. They come for all of us in the responses to our hello. Our lives are linked securely to others by the common footbridges of empathic acts.

When our self-confidence is low, we may even embellish common acts, seeing in them glimpses of greater things. One pastor said, "I got a letter from Jesus today. It was a letter from a woman who has given all she earned from her part-time job for the remodeling of the church.

Let me tell you, that was uplifting, a letter from Jesus, helping me smile a little more with people during difficult times, and helping me have energy for making decisions on things we all know little about." Is this exaggeration? Unreality? No. It is the capacity for reverent imagination, for seeing the holy in the common, which sustains our lives.

Being Open to Responses

At the very least, pastors, spouses, and congregations need to be receptive to empathic responses. That is not always easy to do. In these pages we have seen situations where emotionally scarred couples and congregations have hidden their need for sustaining responses. Opening themselves to the care of others means to risk being injured again. Moreover, opening themselves leaves them vulnerable to injuries from the inside as well, namely from the resurrection of humiliating memories of times when they felt stupid, needy, or angry with themselves. At the worse, individuals and congregations live as between two worlds, one dead and the other powerless to be born.

We need people around us who understand our sensitivities, who do not get impatient with us and either try to knock down our door of privacy or turn away in disgust. How life-enhancing it is for us to be embraced by others who know how to get close but not too close, who sense the balance that is comfortable for us. And yet we need to make an effort, too. We need to risk a bit, to try opening up a little so that we encourage others' efforts in wanting to be with us.

Some pastors, spouses, and parishes harbor a secret feeling that no one could really reassure them. There is no one they idealize, for example, no one whose words wrap around their heart and give them peace. They see everyone as having feet of clay, their own limitations and weaknesses. "How can I find comfort in another person who is basically struggling with the same things I am?" one clergy wife asked.

That is a tough question. The problem with it is the assumption that we can be soothed only by people whom we experience as superior to us, who have a quality of character that is beyond ours and the ordinary. If this were true, then Jesus would have emotionally relied upon God only. Because he was the Son of God, everyone was his inferior, so how could he turn to them for the comfort his soul cried for? And yet he did. He leaned upon the loving support of his disciples. He let them know the depth of his worries and sought a good word from them. He needed them by him in the Garden of

Gethsemane to ease his fright and steel his will. Looking at Jesus, maybe we can humble ourselves enough to accept the human support that others offer us. When we do that, we may be surprised at how powerfully reassuring the offered acts of others can be. Blessed are those who hunger and thirst for empathy.

THIRTEEN
Mind Mending

I N AGONIZING MOMENTS, we tend to yearn for a supportive touch more than a sensitive explanation. When
we fell down physically at the playground or socially at the dance, we
ran to mother for a comforting embrace. But if we were fortunate
enough to have an empathic mother, she usually gave us an explanation
too. As she stroked she also spoke, interspersing little lessons of why
we had the mishap, what our feelings were all about, and how we
could make things better. Those simple explanations strengthened us.
They gave us something in our mind to hold on to, some way to make
sense of, if not control, what was happening to us. Mother's legacy to
us was both her touch and her telling. With mother we both received
empathic understanding and were helped to empathically understand.
Both were vital in shaping our feelings of security in the world.

An experience of feeling understood becomes more concrete and
solid within pastor, spouse, and congregation when they understand
those experiences. Explanations and interpretations lift individuals' or
parishes' experiences into the realm of conscious thought, allowing
them to recall and lean upon those supportive experiences when
needed. As Charles Talbot said later in therapy, "I'm seeing now how
Janice has been supportive of me in many little ways that I simply
took for granted. I brushed them off, looking for something bigger.
But those small signs of caring kept me going, even when I minimized
them. I'm thankful for the ways she's been a good wife to me and a
good mother to our children."

Explanations can also strengthen trust in the bond that has been established between one's self and supportive others. As Rev. Janice Talbot was later able to say to Charles, "I know, now, that when you get angry at me, it's because I'm so important to you, and that helps me not feel so cut off from you and alone when it happens."

Explanations also help the individual or parish handle their own feelings more adequately. As Charles began to understand the meaning of his rage toward Janice, he was able to stop his own mounting self-doubts and to reduce his internal tension.

Explanations are also gratifying. We can feel proud about knowing, invigorated by the new understandings we feel we now possess and can use. We can feel uplifted by the power of explanations and insights, immersed in the wisdom of humankind that both grounds and enlarges our being. We can feel the bliss of belonging when we are in the know, participating with colleagues, familiar and imagined, who share similar perspectives.

EXPLANATIONS THAT HEAL

The ultimate purpose of explanations should be to support, nourish, and restore the self of pastor, spouse, and parish. Explanations are means of healing grace when they convey empathy, carry the experience of empathy, and create empathy. Every time a pastor, for example, decides to make an interpretation to the parish about parish life, the ultimate purpose should be to speak in such a way that the congregation feels itself empathically understood, while also having its own empathic understanding of its self and others broadened. That can be done in a variety of ways.

The pastor may resonate with the parish and remind them of what they already know but have forgotten. "Remember the last time this church was involved in a missionary outreach venture? We really felt great about ourselves. That can happen again." Or the pastor may offer an explanation that brings into clarity something the parish has known implicitly but vaguely. "This congregation certainly is not falling apart, but it does seem to be mourning. There's a subtle communal sadness around here about the loss of your former pastor that isn't talked about much." Then again, the pastor may convey empathy for the parish and strive to enhance the parish's own empathic understanding by offering explanations with new insights for the parish. "This congregation has a mistaken picture of itself. Measured against the world's standards, it is small and poor, but measured against God's standards it is a jewel of faithfulness and care." Explanations can mend minds that have forgotten, have been confused, or have dwelt in dark despair. The purpose is not education for education's sake, but education for the strengthening of hope and compassion. "Then I will see face to face," said Saint Paul (1 Cor. 13:12), and that meant all the difference in the character and quality of his life.

EMPATHIC UNDERSTANDING

In order for a pastor, spouse, or parish to be helped by an explanation, two primary conditions must be met. First, individuals or parishes need to be sufficiently cohesive. Explanations can hurt us in the process of healing us. When we look inside and try to face courageously what shapes our thinking and behavior, we are exposing our self. We risk losing our cherished ideas about our self as we confront our longings, defenses, and angers. We have to be secure enough within our self to face these realizations about who we are.

A hypersensitive individual or parish is limited in the capacity to endure the threat of injury that such self-exposure presents. When most of one's emotional energy is devoted to holding the self together, little energy is available for the taxing work of personal soul-searching.

Lack of attention to the quality of an individual's or group's self-cohesion accounts for much of the failure of conflict resolution approaches. Such approaches are often based on the assumption that the parties involved will be able to use their head, to rationally reflect with some calmness. The approaches expect that the parties will be able to understand the other's point of view, to put themselves in each other's shoes. The approaches anticipate that the parties will have the capacity to work cooperatively and fairly toward fulfillment of everyone's needs.

Struggling pastors, spouses, and parishes typically lack these capacities. Lacking a firm, cohesive self, they tend to act impulsively and defensively. They can tolerate no view other than their own, at least not for very long. And they desperately struggle to get their own pressing needs met. Such individuals are not unethical or irresponsible. They lack the internal capacities to endure tension, to risk taking the other's viewpoint, and to live with something less than what they feel they need.

When individuals, couples, or parishes are inwardly weak, they may rely more on apology than explanation for peaceful resolution of conflicted relationships. Apologies are often the beginnings of reconciliation, but apologies are not efforts to come to new understandings. A clergy couple frightened by their fighting may try to soothe the waters with apologies, rather than with face-to-face examinations and explanations that may cause further storms. Anxious pastors and parishes may try to skirt unresolved difficulties by lacing apologies with promises to try harder. At best, apologies are completed by explanations. For vulnerable selves, they are substitutes for explanations.

The second condition necessary for the broadening of a pastor, spouse, or parish's understanding is that explanations must stretch but not stress. Explanations should allow individuals or parishes sufficient self-recognition and self-understanding, but in a form that compensates for the exposure they suffer. For example, when Jesus spoke to the people, he did not employ a denouncing prophetic style for exposing the people to self-understanding. The prophets nagged their audiences into knowing themselves. Jesus, in contrast, told stories and invited the listeners to see themselves as the central characters. A man was beaten and robbed. He was not like us. Two prominent people from among us passed him by. But a foreigner, from outside us, stopped and aided him. Who was the true neighbor? Go and do likewise. Here we are led to recognize our overly rigid needs for keeping only to our own kind, and how that sort of behavior can be destructive not only to the other but to ourselves. At the same time, the parable form allows us to maintain a degree of self-respect even while we understand the limits of our supposed self-righteousness. The point is that explanations are empathic and healing when they employ tolerable forms of self-recognition.

Protecting Empathic Capacities

Pastors, spouses, and congregations are always just a step and a half away from trouble. Firm as our selves might be, we are perpetually vulnerable to fragmentation. Regardless of how skilled a pastor is in the practice of ministry, or a spouse is in getting along with parishioners and pastor partner, or a parish is in managing its affairs, unless they are skilled in self-care they can be seriously thrown off balance by injurious words and deeds. Care of one's self is not sinful but humanly basic. That applies most particularly to protecting one's capacity for empathic understanding.

After being exposed repeatedly to distorted or abusive statements, for example, even firmly cohesive individuals and congregations are in danger of regressing. Unable to sustain their equilibrium, they may respond with comments and criticisms that aim to obliterate offending others. Explanations then seek to expel. Interpretations attempt to intimidate. Understanding gives way to labeling. Confrontation degenerates into combat. As pastor, spouse, and parish interact, they must be on guard against the erosion of their own cohesion and esteem, where they regress to archaic levels of acting and reasoning. Unfortunately, certain explanations and interpretations represent the most dehumanizing features of rage toward others.

Formulating New Explanations

Even though new self-realizations are painful at times, the whole process of self-understanding can be reassuring, fostering feelings of competence and an increased ability to regulate one's internal tensions. A new world opens, along with new feelings for one's self and others.

Hopefully some new explanations can slip into the privacy of the clergy couple's bedroom. These explanations can be based upon a deepened appreciation for the need to maintain self-cohesion via empathic responses from others. Hopefully new explanations will enter ecclesiastical discussions as well. Through increasing numbers of clergy seminars and pastoral articles, ministers can begin to think of the parish as a group self with a unique history of selfobject needs, satisfactions, and injuries. Explanations grounded in empathic understanding of self can be redemptive for the eternal triangle—and for the wider world.

FOURTEEN
People Making

WE HAVE SEEN THAT WHEN pastors, spouses, or congregations are too needy, depressed, or angry, they are unable to respond with maximal empathy. When that happens, not only do those who need them suffer, but *they* suffer. We become a firm, well-integrated person or parish when we gradually regain the capacity to serve as someone's selfobject. We feel the pleasure of being our best self when extending our care to another. We feel warmed by living out the ultimate value given us by Jesus to love our neighbor as ourself. We feel the satisfaction of participating with cherished others whose existences are made meaningful through service. Health ensues for us and others when we respond empathically. Responding empathically is people making.

THE GROUNDS FOR RESPONDING

Throughout these pages the term *empathy* has been allowed to define itself from the human situations described. You implicitly know that empathy means feeling with another person, putting yourself in their shoes. *Empathy* comes from the German *einfühlen,* "to feel," or more accurately, to find one's way into another's experience. That is what we have been trying to do with pastors, spouses, and congregations, to feel and find our way into their way of experiencing life.

Responding empathically to another, therefore, requires resonating with that person or parish so that in our body as well as in our thoughts we sense something of what they are inwardly experiencing and needing. Responding empathically is not based on sympathy, which has been folksily defined as "your hurt in my heart." We can sympathize with another without understanding them. Instead, our responses are best motivated and shaped by our deep, vibrating comprehension of the self of pastors, spouses, and congregations, where we share, for a time, their inner subjective realities.

In most of our relationships we are more geared to action of some sort than to patiently immersing ourselves in another's inner world. We want to "do" rather than deeply listen, to "make it better" for another rather than feel with another. A humanizing change occurs for us, however, when we strive to convert our assertive energies into empathic efforts. First and foremost should be an attunement to the other, an emotional resonance that results in understanding, which then leads to empathic mirroring, idealizing, or alterego responses.

PRACTICING EMPATHY

It is healthy for us to practice empathy even when we don't feel motivated to do so. When we are hurting inside, we can try to be functionally empathic; that is, we can try to resonate sufficiently with others so we can functionally cooperate. It is no small step toward healing marital strife, for example, when we begin to talk civilly to our spouse about arrangements for the day. Acknowledging that the spouse needs the car, or reaffirming prior plans to have the church deacons over to the house for coffee, expresses a level of empathic consideration that can lead to reconciliation. Similarly, a parish that continues to attend church and contribute adequately even when disappointed in the pastor or spouse, extends empathic regard that keeps the parish self stable and pastoral ties redeemable. Each act of empathy heals, and each practice of empathy contributes to self-growth.

It is also healthy for us to broaden the limits of our empathy. When we are in a reasonably cohesive state, we can try to extend empathy for people who are unlikable, who have limited ability to get the gifts of support. The fact is that pastors, spouses, and congregations need empathic responses the most when they are the least likable. In this situation we must be thoughtful about the matter of forgiveness.

Forgiveness of people who are unlikable may be an empathic response. They may be yearning for reinclusion into the human family, and into God's care, which a word of forgiveness can grant. But our forgiving is not primary over our understanding. Forgiveness can be a quick substitute for understanding, or an actual way of trying to distance our self from the unlikable other through apparent kindness. Forgiving can get us off the hook of really knowing and responding in depth to a person or parish that is unattractive if not repulsive to us. A clergy spouse once said, "It's easier to get forgiveness in the church than understanding." Acts themselves are not empathic. Human and religious acts are empathic and healing only when the person feels understood and supported.

HEADS-UP RESPONSES

By empathically entering into the life of a pastor, spouse, or parish, we sense their needs for mirroring, idealizing, or alterego responses. We also sense the prevailing intensity of those needs depending upon the current state of self-cohesion of the individual, couple, or group. As empathic selfobject figures, we try to respond accordingly.

A husband may become aware, for example, that his wife thrives principally on affirmations from others. As a loving partner, he tries to remember to offer such mirroring responses when an occasion arises. He also empathically senses the appropriate magnitude and form of those responses. A mature spouse may feel patronized by over-effusive praise. More quiet or intellectual recognition of excellent work may feel more appropriate to the spouse, fortifying the spouse's inner confidence. Mirroring, idealizing, or alterego responses are unempathic, and thus effectively useless, unless they are packaged in words and gestures appropriate for the individual's (or group's) state of self.

If the wife feels cut to the quick by a criticism in the parish, and her self-esteem plummets, she may yearn for a more direct, intense mirroring response that will help overcome the pain of rejection. The wife may want to hear: "You've been doing a great job. Most of the people think you're terrific. I certainly do. You're too bright and creative to let this get you down." In other words, a person who feels injured depends more upon the support of others. Selfobject needs are normal for all, but become more pressing the more an individual's self-cohesion is threatened.

Even in this situation, however, the husband's response to the depleted spouse needs to be monitored empathically. The wife may not want him to be a rousing cheerleader, but may want him to allow her expressions of self-pity, or want him to enter into her pain and frustration. The yearning is for the presence of someone who understands.

That understanding may be shown verbally or nonverbally. Sitting silently holding the spouse's hand can be as sustaining as a litany of reassurances. Often, an understanding presence is all that is needed. Embraced by the partner's resonating spirit and leaning upon his supportive affirmations, the wife may well recover her temporarily lost state of well-being.

But what if the wife begins to slip into serious self-preoccupation? What if she wants her husband to make all decisions, wants to stay home, wants him to make excuses for her avoidance of the church? In short, what happens if she begins to seriously fragment? In those situations, the spouse's responses are still shaped by one overarching principle: He is committed to the health and preservation of his spouse's self. What he decides to do is determined by his empathic assessment as to what will protect and promote her inner core. While he will convey understanding for the meaning the wife is trying to get him to see, he will primarily attend in this situation to the state of the spouse's self. Consequently, he may not give primary heed to what his wife claims will feel good to her. He may not take at face value her claim that "there's no problem," or (at the other extreme) that "everything is hopeless." For the well-being of his wife, he looks beyond gratifying her immediate wishes and beyond her perception of the situation.

At crisis times we must be a selfobject-in-action.[16] The cohesion of the partner may become so vulnerable that we must step in as a temporary substitute and help the other function in ways he or she is unable to presently. We do this not out of superiority but out of commitment to preserve the other's core. Responding empathically, therefore, does not mean just giving what the self wants. It means responding with what the self requires, based upon careful observation and understanding of the person, and based upon a commitment to keeping that person whole and healthy.

When persons or parishes are in a state of severe fragmentation, the need for empathic action is central. For instance, Rev. Dan Weber, Julie Weber, and Grace Church were all deteriorating. They faced the danger of increased fragmentation and the possibility of total disintegration—spiritually, morally, socially, emotionally, and physically. This pastor, spouse, congregation and their relationships required immediate shoring up. Any intervention by a denominational leader or pastoral consultant would need to be in the nature of crisis management. The central effort would be to ward off the escalating deterioration of each self and of their relationships. The therapeutic helper, therefore, would provide structure, direction, and encouragement for the parties, who could not do so for themselves. This would be done in such a way that pastor, spouse, and congregation could feel empathically cared for.

This would not be a time for helping them empathically understand themselves. A denominational official who sought counseling for Rev. Dan Weber, Julie Weber, and Grace Church meant well when he stated, "The first thing to do is to get them to understand themselves." Such a point of departure would have been therapeutically inadvisable. Instead, what they needed was to have someone empathically understand their desperate plight and help them do something to hold body and soul together. This was the vital starting point of self-restoration. Inasmuch as the boundaries of a fragmenting pastor, spouse, or parish tend to shrink to where capacities for self-observation, tolerance for complex ideas, and receptivity to divergent viewpoints are limited (if not absent), attempting to foster understanding via explanations fails to address the immediate issues of self-survival.

Neither was this a time for prompting the parties to respond empathically. Depleted selves have reduced abilities for resonating with others. They have enough trouble holding their own selves together. Encouraging depleted selves to forgive, or to "do unto others," or to "empty thy self" or to "look at the log in your own eye," imposes dictates that cannot be adequately met. The failure to fulfill such moralistic dictates is experienced as a further blow to self-esteem. Moreover, those who point a finger rather than offer a hand to a struggling soul often incur the latter's wrath. What is lost is a potentially sustaining response that the individual or parish so sorely needs.

CONCLUSION
The Hope for Restoration

JANICE AND CHARLES TALBOT smiled warmly as they entered my office. They seemed relaxed, even playful. "I feel like a man who has both perspective and patience," said Charles. "I'm sustained by knowing my history, by seeing the ups and downs, and by knowing the ups will come again. There's a kind of wisdom I feel fortified by, this wider, deeper perspective on things. And I have more patience with myself, and with others. Something more permanent has lodged inside me."

"I feel something of the same," added Janice. "I'm not as vulnerable to his moods anymore. I still want to feel we're a team, but I'm much more confident that I can do my ministry by myself. I've gotten a lot better at telling the church no when it makes too many demands on me. And you know what? The church didn't get angry when I did it. In fact, they have accommodated to my schedule. It's been a growing experience for us all. I'm thankful that relationships are better at home and in the church, especially since I had serious doubts that anything would ever change."

I was glad also, for them and for the parish. And I was convinced again that once we see the world differently, we inhabit a new world. Once we connect with each other with empathic understanding, we relate to each other in new, redeeming ways. Then it is that the eternal triangle becomes a reflection of God's grace.

Notes

1. To understand the self of pastor, clergy spouse, and congregation we turn to a body of clinical work and reflection called self psychology. Self psychology is the name by which the insights of the late Heinz Kohut, and the contributions of other like-minded colleagues, have come to be known in the areas of psychoanalysis, psychology, and pastoral counseling. A reader wishing to know more about Kohut and self psychology would best begin with Paul Ornstein's introduction to volume 1 of Kohut's *The Search for the Self*. Charles Strozier's introduction to Kohut's *Self Psychology and the Humanities: Reflections on a New Psychoanalytic Approach* is also illuminating. Chapter 2 of my book, *Pastor and Parish: The Psychological Core of Ecclesiastical Conflicts,* also presents an overview of the self psychology perspective.

2. R. L. Randall, *Pastor and Parish: The Psychological Core of Ecclesiastical Conflicts* (New York: Human Sciences Press, 1988), 92.

3. Part of a statement of the Ministry Studies Board of the United Presbyterian Church.

4. G. A. Smith, *The Book of Isaiah* (London: Hodder & Stoughton, 1927), 262.

5. M. K. Bower, *Conflicts of the Clergy* (New York: Thomas Nelson & Sons, 1963), 1.

6. M. G. Taylor, "Two-person Career or Two-Career Marriage?" *The Christian Ministry* 8, no. 1 (1977): 18–20.

7. J. Wright, "Notes from a Pastor's Husband." *The Christian Century* (January 1986): 17.

8. B. J. Niswander, "Clergy Wives of the New Generation." *Pastoral Psychology* (Spring 1982): 160–69.

9. These descriptions of needed balance are my borrowings from a pervasive theme of the great theologian Reinhold Niebuhr. See, for example: *The Self and the Dramas of History* (New York: Charles Scribner's Sons, 1955).

10. M. B. Oden, "Stress and Purpose: Clergy Spouses Today." *The Christian Century* (April 20, 1988): 403–4.

11. D. R. Mace and V. C. Mace, *What's Happening to Clergy Marriages?* (Nashville: Abingdon, 1980).

12. P. Valeriano, "A Survey of Ministers' Wives." *Leadership* 2 (Fall 1981): 64–73.

13. Oden, "Stress and Purpose," 402–4.

14. Randall, *Pastor and Parish,* 98–102.

15. While this scenario is not unlike a scene in the movie *Moonstruck,* written by John Patrick Shanley, it also is remarkably similar to an actual counseling conversation.

16. H. L. Muslin and E. R. Val, *The Psychotherapy of the Self* (New York: Brunner/Mazel, 1987), 61–95.

Glossary

The following terms, drawn from the self psychology of Heinz Kohut and others, are used throughout this book.

alterego need
: The normal need of people to experience that others are like them (their alterego). The assurance of being surrounded by self-same others contributes to a feeling of being human and of belonging. An insecure person may demand that others be just like the person in order for the person to feel normal or to be assured of belonging. (*See* archaic, idealizing need, mirroring need, selfobject.)

archaic
: Adjective describing the immature forms of alterego, idealizing, and mirroring needs.

cohesion
: (*See* self-cohesion.)

empathy
: The capacity of individuals to sense the needs of others and to respond in sensitively appropriate ways; the capacity to enter into the world of others and to experience how life is for them. (*See* empathically responding persons.)

empathically responding persons
: The kind of people each of us needs in order for us to feel strong and secure in-

side. The empathic responses of others to our selfobject needs become the basis for our firm self-cohesion and positive self-esteem. (*See* empathy, self-cohesion, self-esteem, selfobject.)

fragmentation The sense of falling apart and needing to be shored up. This sense can be brief or can persist over a long period of time, even a lifetime. During such periods, a person is unusually vulnerable and sensitive to disappointments and criticisms.

group self The nature of a group to have a core self and to need its alterego, idealizing, and alterego yearnings met, just as an individual does. In the presence of empathic responses, the group, like the individual, can feel harmonious and balanced inside. It can enjoy firm self-cohesion and positive self-esteem and, out of this fullness, can respond empathically to others.

idealizing need The normal need of people to feel connected to persons they admire and see as a source of soothing or power. Feeling linked with such idealized figure(s) gives a person a sense of calmness or strength. An insecure person may demand that the idealized figure be constantly available and never show flaws, for the insecure person relies upon the idealized figure to keep the insecure self from fragmenting. (*See* alterego need, fragmentation, mirroring need, selfobject.)

mirroring need The normal need of persons to be admired and seen as special by others. Responses to a person's need for mirroring recognition lead to healthy pursuit of one's goals and ambitions. An insecure person may demand that others applaud or affirm his or her accomplishments, lest the person become fragmented. (*See* alterego need, fragmentation, idealizing need, selfobject.)

rage response   A person's response when his or her mirroring, idealizing, or alterego needs are not met as expected or demanded. These responses range widely, from the passing disgust a person might experience when he or she feels ignored, for example, to actual murder of the insulting figure. (*See also* withdrawal response.)

self   The sense a person has that he or she is something more than parts, mental processes, or roles. The self is the core of each person's being, which is experienced as "me," as one's essential personhood. To develop and maintain a healthy sense of self, each person needs empathic responses from others to the self's basic mirroring, idealizing, and alterego needs. (*See* alterego need, idealizing need, mirroring need, self-cohesion.)

self-cohesion   The strength, harmony, and vitality of a person's sense of self. A person who possesses positive and reliable self-esteem, and whose self does not fragment in the face of threats, has firm self-cohesion. The person who lacks reliable self-esteem and is always on the verge of falling apart has weak self-cohesion. There is a wide spectrum between these two extremes. All persons normally fluctuate between them.

self-esteem   The general sense of well-being when a person enjoys firm self-cohesion as his or her mirroring, idealizing, and alterego needs are empathically responded to.

selfobject   The normal tendency of each person to experience the other as part of the person's very self. The other becomes the self's object, an extension of the self; thus the term *selfobject.* Needing others to be resonating parts of one's world is not abnormal, nor just a stage that will be outgrown. We all need others to act as our selfobjects throughout life. Empathic responses from persons we make our selfobjects keep our self cohesive and our self-esteem positive. (*See* alterego need, idealizing need, mirroring need, self-cohesion.)

withdrawal response

A person's response when his or her mirroring, idealizing, or alterego needs are not met as expected or demanded. Withdrawal responses exist on a wide spectrum—from quiet pouting when one feels slighted, for example, to a psychotic comatose state. (*See also* rage response.)

Selected Bibliography

Bailey, M. F. "Choosing between Substance and Shadow: The Many Possible Roles of the Minister's Spouse." *The Christian Century* (January 1986): 10–13.

Bouma, M. L. "Ministers' Wives: The Walking Wounded." *Leadership* 1 (1980): 51–63.

Bower, M. K. *Conflicts of the Clergy.* New York: Thomas Nelson & Sons, 1963.

Fitchett, G., ed. "Religion and the Self Psychology of Heinz Kohut: A Memorial Symposium." *Journal of Supervision and Training in Ministry* 5 (1982): 89–205.

Gerkin, C. V. *The Living Human Document: Re-Visioning Pastoral Counseling in a Hermeneutical Mode.* Nashville: Abingdon Press, 1984.

Goldberg, A., ed. *Advances in Self Psychology: With Summarizing Reflections by Heinz Kohut.* New York: International Universities Press, 1980.

———. *The Future of Psychoanalysis: Essays in Honor of Heinz Kohut.* New York: International Universities Press, 1983.

Homans, P. "Introducing the Psychology of the Self and Narcissism into the Study of Religion." *Religious Studies Review* 7 (July 1981): 193–99.

Houts, D. C. "Marriage Counseling with Clergy Couples." *Pastoral Psychology* 30 (Spring 1982): 141–49.

Kohut, H. *The Analysis of the Self.* New York: International Universities Press, 1971.

———. *How Does Analysis Cure?* Edited by A. Goldberg, with P. Stepansky. Chicago: University of Chicago Press, 1984.

———. *The Restoration of the Self.* New York: International Universities Press, 1977.

———. *The Search for the Self: Selected Writings of Heinz Kohut, 1950–1978.* 2 vols. Edited by P. H. Ornstein. New York: International Universities Press, 1978.

———. *Self Psychology and the Humanities: Reflections on a New Psychoanalytic Approach.* Edited by C. B. Strozier. New York: W. W. Norton & Company, 1985.

Mace, D. R., and V. C. Mace. "Marriage Enrichment for Clergy Couples." *Pastoral Psychology* 30 (Spring 1982): 151–59.

Meloy, J. R. "Narcissistic Psychopathology and the Clergy." *Pastoral Psychology* (1986): 50–55.

Miriam, E., ed. *The Kohut Seminars on Self Psychology and Psychotherapy with Adolescents and Young Adults.* New York: W. W. Norton & Company, 1987.

Muslin, H. L., and E. R. Val. *The Psychotherapy of the Self.* New York: Brunner/Mazel, 1987.

Nelson, J. B. *Embodiment: An Approach to Sexuality and Christian Theology.* Minneapolis: Augsburg, 1978.

Niswander, B. J. "Clergy Wives of the New Generation." *Pastoral Psychology* 30 (Spring 1982): 160–69.

Nyberg, K. "Whatever Happened to Ministers' Wives?" *The Christian Century* (February 7, 1979): 151–52.

Oden, M. B. "Stress and Purpose: Clergy Spouses Today." *The Christian Century* (April 20, 1988): 402–4.

Presnell, W. B. "The Minister's Own Marriage." *Pastoral Psychology* 25 (Summer 1977): 272–81.

Randall, R. L. "The Legacy of Kohut for Religion and Psychology." *Journal of Religion and Health* 23 (Summer 1984): 106–14.

———. *Pastor and Parish: The Psychological Core of Ecclesiastical Conflicts.* New York: Human Sciences Press, 1988.

———. *Putting the Pieces Together: Guidance from a Pastoral Psychologist.* New York: Pilgrim Press, 1986.

———. "Religious Ideation of a Narcissistically Disturbed Individual." *Journal of Pastoral Care* 30 (March 1976): 35–45.

———. "Self Psychology in Pastoral Counseling." *Journal of Religion and Health* 28 (Spring 1989): 7–15.

———. "Soteriological Dimensions in the Work of Heinz Kohut." *Journal of Religion and Health* 19 (Summer 1980): 83–91.

Rediger, G. L. "Narcissism." *Church Management* (March 1980): 8–9.

Troost, D. P. "The Minister's Family: People without a Pastor." *Reformed Review* (1978): 75–77.

Valeriano, P. "A Survey of Ministers' Wives." *Leadership* 2 (Fall 1981): 64–73.

Warner, J., and J. Carter. "Loneliness, Marital Adjustment and Burnout in Pastoral and Lay Persons." *Journal of Psychology and Theology* 12 (1984): 125–31.

Index

89069